from

ESTEE'S

KITCHEN

OY VEY VEGAN
cookbook

By Estee Raviv

Creator of *From Estee's Kitchen*

FOOD PHOTOGRAPHY
Estee Raviv

PORTRAIT PHOTOGRAPHY
Craig Sklar and Kayla Casebeer

DESIGN
Kristin McCleerey, K Brand Studio

from
ESTEE'S
KITCHEN

Oy Vey Vegan Cookbook
by Estee Raviv

Edited by Orian Raviv and
Brian Buttleman

ISBN: 978-0-578-18501-9

Printed in South Korea
by Star Print Brokers, Inc.
Bellevue, WA
StarPrintBrokers.com

Ordering Information:
Quantity sales. Special discounts
are available on quantity purchases
by corporations, associations, and
others. For permission requests or
ordering information, visit:
www.esteeskitchen.com/contact.

For bonus recipes, please visit:
www.esteeskitchen.com/subscribe.

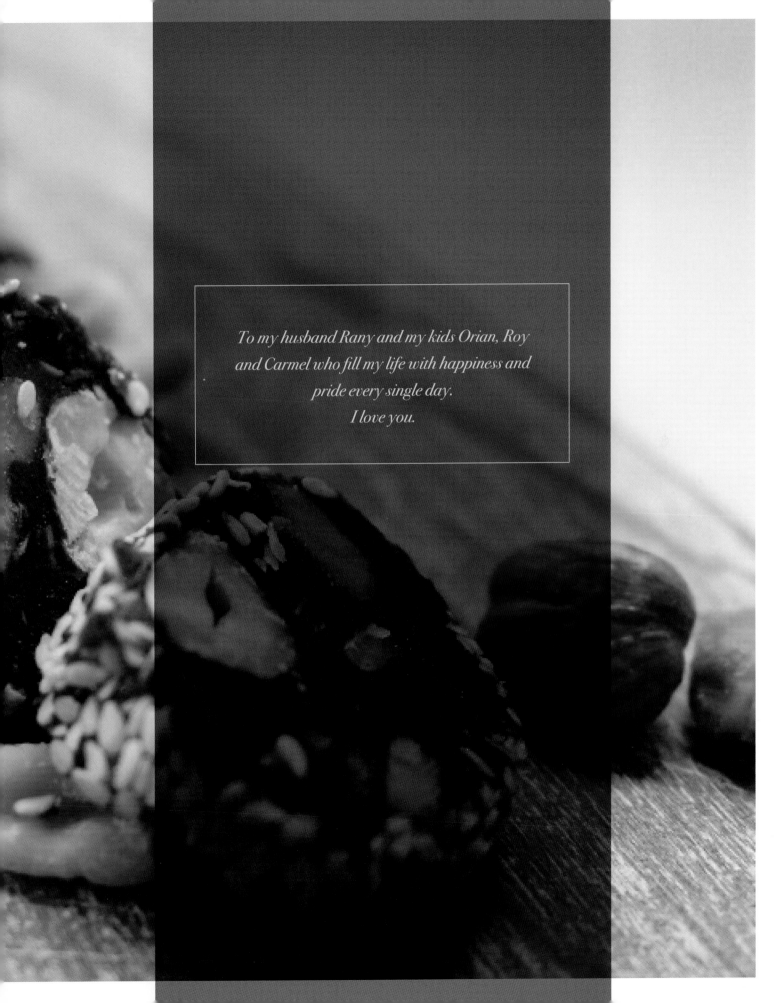

*To my husband Rany and my kids Orian, Roy
and Carmel who fill my life with happiness and
pride every single day.
I love you.*

Contents

For more recipes From Estee's Kitchen, visit:
www.esteeskitchen.com

ABOUT *Estee*

My love for cooking and healthy food has been inspired by a life filled with art, travel, world culture and experiences, all shared with family and friends.

My name is Estee. Born in Israel, I grew up on the sandy shores of the Mediterranean Sea. When I was young, my meals were influenced by flavors of the Middle East, along with my Jewish heritage and the Eastern European traditions of my Romanian mother—an incredible cook and hostess—and my Polish father. My culinary experiences were further enriched by my family's travels around the world, exposing me to wonderfully diverse foods and traditions.

I thank those travels in part for my life-long love of art and creative expression. My background in graphic design, gemology and art studies led me to owning a successful, high-end, custom jewelry business in Israel. After my move to the United States with my husband and children, I continued to work with polymer clay and photography (yes, the recipe photos in this book are my own!).

Throughout it all, cooking has always been my passion and path to relaxation. It provides a creative outlet much like my artwork—with delicious returns! Whether hosting guests from all over the world or teaching cooking classes in my home, I've found ways to spread my love for healthy, creative cooking. It's always inspiring to share my knowledge of cooking with others that may not be as knowledgeable or experienced. I try to inspire a kind of culinary fearlessness. The kitchen should be a place to try new things. It's great fun developing delicious vegan recipes that anyone can enjoy. Together this book and my blog, From Estee's Kitchen, offer the perfect way to "spread the love."

I believe that each and every one of us eats with their eyes first, so the presentation of each individual dish and the book as a whole is as important as the recipes. I enjoyed taking the time to style, plate and photograph all the dishes myself. The whole process helped me discover and share a part of my inner self.

Healthy food and a healthy lifestyle is a big part of who I am, and I am honored to share this with you. The phrase "you are what you eat," defines one of my strongest held values. When you eat right, exercise and feel good about yourself, you are able to reflect that positive outlook onto the world.

Cooking healthy is not necessarily difficult, it is a matter of choice and priorities. There is no need to be a chemist or a chef to make good food. If you eat plant-based food that remains close to its original form, you will be repaid with a healthy mind and body.

I chose to title my book Oy Vey Vegan because oftentimes, people's first reaction to vegan cooking is "Oy Vey!" or an equivalent "Oh no!" In this book, you'll find that vegan food is not something to shy away from, but rather something to embrace because it can be, and is, so tasty and does wonders for your health.

Today I live with my husband and three children in Portland, Oregon. Health-conscious myself, I teach my kids about the benefits of good, healthy meals and expose them to as much variety as possible. I developed all the recipes found here and on From Estee's Kitchen, and my ever-supportive family has contributed greatly as willing taste-testers.

This cookbook and From Estee's Kitchen allow me to do good things not only for my own family but also for others. Thanks and hope you enjoy the book!

Estee

BREAKFAST
&
Brunch

Yield

1 *serving*

 GF

1	kiwi, peeled and cut in half
1	medium apple, about 1 cup
1	small pear, about 1/2 cup
10	mint leaves
+	juice of 1/2 lemon
1	celery stalk
1/2 C	vanilla almond milk
1 TSP	pure maple syrup
+	ice (optional)

ENERGY BOOST SHAKE

This energy booster shake is a lovely way to start the day! Loaded with vitamin C and fiber, this nutritional shake is great to make for your kids. They will love this treat on a hot summer day, after school or for breakfast.

Blend all ingredients in a blender until smooth and creamy. Drink immediately.

Yield

2-3 *servings*

 GF

1 1/4 C   carrots
1 C   steamed or fresh beets
1 TSP   (or less) fresh ginger root
10   fresh mint leaves
1/4 C   apple
1   stalk of celery
2 TBSP   pure maple syrup
+   juice of 1 lemon
1 C   vanilla almond milk
1/4 C   water
+   ice (optional)

RED GOODNESS SHAKE

Want to boost your body with nutrients quickly? This is a good way to do it! It's quick, tasty and full of vitamins. Drink it first thing in the morning and you're done. You'll feel very energetic, satisfied and ready to start your day.

Fruit and veggie shakes are a great way to consume your daily amount of required nutrients. It's naturally sweet and contains antioxidants and fiber. Give it a try and incorporate it into your daily morning routine.

Blend all ingredients in a blender until smooth and creamy. Drink immediately.

Yield

1 *serving*

1	frozen banana
1	celery stalk
1 TSP	fresh turmeric root
+	juice of 1/2 lemon
10	fresh mint leaves
1/2 C	of kale
1	small pear
1/2 C	vanilla almond milk
+	ice (optional)

BREAKFAST GREEN SHAKE

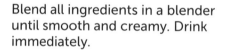

Did you know that turmeric is a powerful medicine that has been used in Chinese and Indian medicine as an anti-inflammatory agent? It can help to reduce rheumatoid arthritis and treat depression, diabetes and cancer. It can also slow skin aging, as well as enhance memory and benefit overall brain health.

Blend all ingredients in a blender until smooth and creamy. Drink immediately.

1 *serving*

1/4 C   gf steel cut oats or gf old fashioned oats
3/4 C   boiling water
1 TSP   chia seeds
1 TSP   flaxseed meal
3-4   walnut halves, chopped
1 TBSP   dried cranberries
+   roasted almond slices
1 TSP   pure maple syrup
+   cinnamon

FAVORITE BREAKFAST OATMEAL

I get asked a lot about my oatmeal breakfast recipe. After years of eating toast with cottage cheese and jam, I realized how bad it was for me.

Since making the change, I feel a lot better. It completely changed my life. If you experience problems with your digestive system, try this for breakfast. Together with a cup of tea, water, or even coffee, you'll quickly feel the benefits and it's very tasty and filling. The crunch of the nuts and the sweetness of the cranberries and pure maple syrup is divine! You'll love it!

Prepare the night before.

In a mason jar, add oats, chia seeds, flaxseed meal and boiling water. Place in the refrigerator.

The next day, microwave for 1 minute and mix. Adjust amount of water added depending on preference of consistency.

Add walnuts, cranberries, almonds, pure maple syrup and cinnamon.

Mix and enjoy.

Yield

9 *pancakes*

2 C   roasted pumpkin purée (I prefer fresh roasted pumpkin but you can also use canned.)
1/2 C   water
1/2 C   vanilla almond milk
1 TSP   vanilla extract
1 TBSP   pure maple syrup
3/4 C   spelt or white flour
1/2 TSP   baking powder
1/2 TSP   baking soda
+   pinch of salt
1 TSP   coconut oil for the pan

PUMPKIN PANCAKES

When pumpkins are in season and just about everywhere you look, I love all the festivities surrounding them. The variety of pumpkins available now is amazing. From green to white to orange to yellow and so many more!

I took my son to the pumpkin patch the other day and bought one of every variety, color, and size. Each one tasted different.

I like to roast pumpkins in the oven and use the flesh as a base for a variety of dishes from savory to sweet. I also like to decorate my kitchen with these beautiful pumpkins.

Take two mixing bowls.

In one, add pumpkin purée, water, almond milk, vanilla extract and pure maple syrup. Mix well.

In the other bowl, add flour, baking powder, baking soda and a pinch of salt. Mix well.

Add the dry ingredients to the wet ingredients. Mix well. Let stand for 15 minutes.

In a nonstick pan, heat coconut oil over medium heat. Using an ice cream scoop, gently pour the batter into the pan. When the edges begin to brown, flip the pancake. Let sit for 5-10 minutes before serving.

8 *servings*

1 TBSP   olive oil
      1   large onion, chopped
      1   package of organic baby
          fresh spinach
          (1 lb/454 g)
      1   package of organic
          sprouted firm tofu
          (14 oz/397 g)
      +   salt
      +   pepper
2 TBSP   nutritional yeast
1 TBSP   sesame seeds
1 TBSP   hemp seeds
    1 C   garbanzo bean flour
    1 C   water
      +   zest of 1 lemon
      +   olive oil spray

Spinach casserole is a great dish to prepare if you are expecting a lot of people or as a brunch item to feed a crowd. The lemon zest brings out the flavors, and the casserole's super smooth texture makes it melts in your mouth.

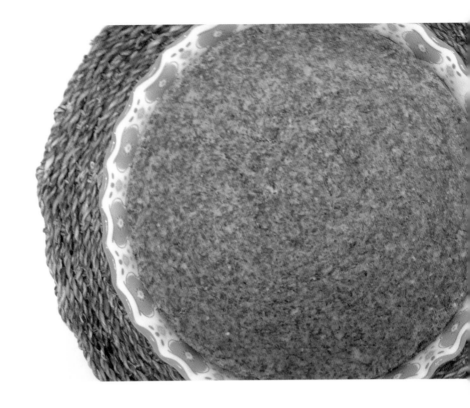

SPINACH CASSEROLE

Heat oven to 375° F.

Spray a round casserole dish with olive oil.

In a nonstick pan on medium heat, add olive oil, onion, salt and pepper. Sauté for a few minutes until onions are translucent. Add spinach and sauté until the spinach is wilted. Set aside.

In a food processor, add tofu, (break the tofu with your hands first), salt, pepper, nutritional yeast, sesame seeds, hemp seeds, garbanzo bean flour, water, and zest of lemon. Blend until smooth.

Add spinach-onion mixture and pulse until combined.

Pour into casserole dish and bake for about 30-45 minutes or until the top starts to get golden.

Let set for at least 20 minutes before serving. It is tasty even at room temperature. I like to drizzle mine with homemade tahini sauce (page 46) and serve along with bulgur tabbouleh salad (page 82).

CHEESE BLINTZES

Yield

14 *servings*

batter:

1 C	almond milk
2 C	water
2 TBSP	melted coconut oil
1 TBSP	vanilla extract
4 TBSP	pure maple syrup
+	pinch of salt
2 C	white flour or spelt flour

cheese filling:

+	silken tofu (15.5 oz/439 g)
1/2 C	vegan cream cheese
1/2 C	pure maple syrup
+	zest and juice of one lemon

topping:

+	powdered sugar
+	strawberries

In a mixing bowl add almond milk, water, oil, vanilla extract, maple syrup and salt. Mix well.

Add flour and a pinch of salt gradually and mix constantly until smooth with no lumps. Let the batter sit for 15-20 minutes while you prepare the filling (you can use an immersion blender).

In a food processor, add all filling ingredients and process until smooth and creamy. Set aside.

Heat a nonstick pan to medium heat. Use a ladle to pour evenly sized blintzes (no need to grease the pan). When the batter begins to bubble and the edges start to turn golden, they're ready to flip. Cook for a couple more minutes on the other side. The blintzes should be golden pale.

assembly:

Lay one blintz on a working surface. Place cheese filling in the middle 1/3 of the blintz, leaving about an inch of space on the top and bottom. First, fold in the sides, then fold the top down. Place seam-side down on a plate. Continue this same process with the rest of the blintzes. Sprinkle with powdered sugar and top with strawberries. Serve warm or cold.

My mom used to make cheese blintzes for us once a week as part of a special "dairy lunch." In Israel, people generally eat their heavier meal at lunch time, and dinner is the lighter meal. I remember how I loved those lunches and looked forward to them every week.

These blintzes are great for breakfast, snack, or dessert. Add your favorite fruits on top or even inside, mixed with the "cheese." You can also drizzle chocolate on top instead of powdered sugar. You can prepare the blintzes the night before and have them ready for breakfast. Just pop them in the microwave for 30 seconds and enjoy.

Yield

7-9 *mini-cakes*

1 TBSP	olive oil
2	leeks, chopped
4	zucchinis, grated
2	flax eggs (mix 2 tbsp flaxseed meal and 6 tbsp water, let sit for 10-15 minutes)
3/4 C	organic spelt flour
+	salt
+	pepper
+	olive oil spray

HEART-SHAPED MINI ZUCCHINI CAKES

Heart-shaped zucchini savory cakes are such a good way to start your Valentine's Day. They are low in fat and loaded with vitamins. Just a few ingredients and super easy to make.

You can also bake this batter in a one-dish casserole—just be aware that this may take more time in the oven.

Leeks always carry dirt, therefore, they need to be soaked. You want to slice into rings first, then separate and place into a large bowl of water. Next, dry in a salad spinner or with a clean towel.

Heat oven to 375° F.

In a nonstick pan on medium heat, add olive oil, leeks, salt and pepper. Sauté until tender. Set aside and let cool.

In a mixing bowl, add the grated zucchinis, leeks, spelt flour, flax eggs, salt and pepper. Mix well.

Line a baking sheet with parchment paper.

Place a heart-shaped cookie cutter on the parchment paper. Wet your hands and ball enough of the zucchini mixture to fill the heart-shaped cutter. Compress it tightly so the mixture fits the shape, then gently lift the cookie cutter. Repeat with the rest of the mixture.

Spray the top with olive oil and bake until golden brown, about 30 minutes.

Let set for about 10-15 minutes before serving.

2-3 *servings*

(GF)

1	package organic sprouted tofu (15.5 oz/439 g)
1 TBSP	yellow curry paste
1/2 TSP	turmeric
3 TBSP	nutritional yeast
2/3 C	almond or soy milk, unsweetened
1 1/2 TBSP	arrowroot
+	salt
+	pepper

Omelets are one of my favorite lunch options. I eat my oatmeal in the morning and then at lunchtime, I like to eat something packed with enough protein to keep me satisfied for the rest of the day. Add a kale salad garnished with avocado, and you'll have an incredibly balanced meal. It is also a great way to lose weight, since you will be full and feel satisfied. Working from home while trying to lose weight can be challenging because you always feel like eating something. Keep your meals balanced and full of nutrition, and you shouldn't have that feeling.

A tofu omelet seasoned with yellow curry is a unique dish with amazing flavors that compliment each other. It is challenging to work with the thick batter, but well worth it once you get the hang of it. Use a nonstick frying-pan, so you won't need to consume any oil.

TOFU OMELET

Add all ingredients to a food processor and blend until very smooth.

Heat a nonstick pan to low heat.

Pour 1 cup of batter into the pan at a time, gently spreading it as much as possible with a spatula—it'll be pretty thick so it may be a little difficult to spread.

When the edges begin to brown, flip the omelet and cook for a couple more minutes until both sides are golden brown.

Serve with avocado and kale salad.

Yield

2-3 *servings*

1 C   chickpea/garbanzo
       bean flour
1 TSP baking powder
2 TBSP nutritional yeast
1 C   water
1 TSP olive oil
1 C   kale, chopped
2   green onions, chopped
+   salt
+   pepper

CHICKPEA & KALE OMELET

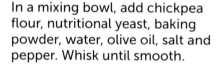

I was first exposed to a chickpea vegan omelet when I was visiting my family in Israel last summer. Lots of coffee shops offer it on their menu, which is awesome. I couldn't believe how flavorful and satisfying it was!

As always, I had to create my own version, so I added kale and onions for an extra layer of flavor! Paired with some vegetables or a salad, it's just perfect.

In a mixing bowl, add chickpea flour, nutritional yeast, baking powder, water, olive oil, salt and pepper. Whisk until smooth.

Add onions and kale. Mix.

On a stove-top, heat a nonstick pan to medium-low heat. Ladle the batter into the pan 1 cup at a time.

Cook until the edges become golden, flip gently and cook through.

Serve warm with your favorite vegetables or salad and drizzle some tahini sauce (page 46).

Yield

6-8 *servings*

(GF)

5 C fresh broccoli or broccolini, chopped
1/2 block silken tofu (7 oz/198.5 g)
1/3 C gf flour blend
2 TBSP nutritional yeast
1/3 C water
2 TBSP yellow mustard
1 TSP onion powder
1 medium onion, thinly chopped
3 cloves garlic, minced
1/3 C olive oil
+ salt
+ pepper

topping:

1/2 C gf bread crumbs
+ olive oil to drizzle on top

Broccoli quiche is a decadent main dish with a crunchy yet soft texture. It is packed with protein (tofu) and antioxidants (broccoli). I used fresh broccolini but you can also use fresh or frozen broccoli that has been thawed. Nutritional yeast gives it a "cheesy" flavor, which goes a long way when combined with mustard and tofu—together they create a wonderful creamy texture. You can also use this batter with a different vegetable, such as cauliflower or roasted pumpkin. My friends and family love it! It is extremely easy to make and so delicious.

BROCCOLI QUICHE

Heat oven to 375° F.

In a mixing bowl, mix all quiche ingredients together with your hands.

assembly:

Grease the bottom of a baking/ pyrex dish with olive oil, pour in the batter, sprinkle with bread crumbs and then drizzle some olive oil on top. Bake for about 50 minutes, until golden brown.

You can also use individual ramekins, like I did, to create individual quiches.

Yield

20 *bars*

4 C	gf oats
1 C	almond butter
1 C	date syrup
1/2 C	maple syrup
1 TSP	cinnamon
1 TBSP	coconut oil
+	dark chocolate, chopped (2 oz/56.5 g)

HOMEMADE GRANOLA BARS

Make your own granola bars once, and trust me, you'll keep making them again and again!

Be in control of what you put into your body. No more processed and unhealthy food! This means you can control the amount of sugar and sodium in your food. With just a few steps and only 20-25 minutes in the oven, it doesn't get easier and quicker than this.

Be creative! Use your favorite nuts, dried fruits, chocolate, or spices. This is a great on-the-go snack that your kids will enjoy. Store them in the fridge in individual bags for easy consumption.

Heat oven to 375° F.

Line a baking sheet with parchment paper.

In a saucepan on low heat, add almond butter, date syrup, maple syrup, cinnamon and coconut oil. Stir until combined. Set aside.

In a large mixing bowl, add the oats.

Pour the sauce over the oats and coat very well.

Add the chopped chocolate and keep mixing until well distributed.

Pour the mixture on to the parchment paper. With wet hands, press the mixture firmly until it's about 1/2" thick.

Bake for about 20-25 minutes, until the edges start to get golden brown. Let cool, cut, and store in individual snack size ziplock bags. An easy, healthy snack for on-the-go.

Yield

11 *biscuits*

(GF)

1 1/2 C	gf oat flour
1 C	brown rice flour
1 C	arrowroot flour
1 C	almond meal
2 TBSP	flaxseed meal
2 TBSP	toasted sesame seeds
2 TBSP	raw sunflower seeds
1 TBSP	salt
1 TSP	baking powder
1 TSP	baking soda
1 TBSP	nutritional yeast
1 TBSP	pure maple syrup
2 TBSP	olive oil
2 C	water

topping:

1 TBSP	nigella seeds
1 TBSP	olive oil

These gluten-free biscuits are amazing. Not only do they melt in your mouth, but they are also so easy to make.

The flavor is mild yet sophisticated. You only need a mixing bowl and a whisk, and you can make them just before serving. They are best when fresh out of the oven. A great breakfast or brunch item, especially if you have gluten-free guests. It is so handy to have a recipe like this that uses ingredients that you already have in your pantry. Be creative, add your favorite nuts or grains.

GLUTEN-FREE BISCUITS

Heat oven to 375° F.

Line a baking sheet with parchment paper.

In a mixing bowl, add the dry ingredients: oat flour, rice flour, arrowroot flour, almond meal, flaxseed, sesame seeds, sunflower, salt, baking powder, baking soda and nutritional yeast. Mix.

In another bowl add the wet ingredients: pure maple syrup, olive oil and water. Mix.

Pour the wet ingredients into the dry ingredients. Mix well.

Measure out the batter using an ice cream scoop, placing evenly sized portions on the parchment paper. Dip the scoop in a cup of warm water before each portion to help keep the batter from sticking.

Brush with olive oil, sprinkle with nigella seeds and bake for about 20 minutes. Serve warm.

HOMEMADE CEREAL

Yield

1	*box of cereal*

1 C	almond flour
1 1/2 C	organic spelt flour
4 TBSP	flaxseed meal
1 1/2 C	wheat bran
1/2 TSP	salt
2 TBSP	coconut oil
3/4 C	pure maple syrup
1/2 C	water

Heat oven to 350° F.

In a food processor, add the dry ingredients: almond flour, spelt flour, flaxseed meal, wheat bran and salt. Pulse a few times.

Then add the coconut oil, maple syrup and water. Pulse again until you get a wet dough mixture.

Line 2 baking sheets with parchment paper.

Divide the dough in half. Sprinkle the parchment paper with spelt flour and also dust the rolling pin. Roll the dough as thin as you can.

Bake in the oven for about 30 minutes, until the dough is dry. Let cool completely and break into pieces with your hands.

Serve with your favorite milk and add some dried blueberries. Store in an air tight container in a cool dry place.

This homemade cereal is addictive! It is even great as a snack with your coffee or tea since it is not too sweet. This cereal is super crunchy and contains natural vitamins.

APPETIZERS, SPREADS
& *Side Dishes*

HUMMUS

Yield

4-6 *servings*

- 3 C dried garbanzo beans soaked overnight, cooked and drained (measurement refers to the cooked beans)
- 1 TSP salt
- 1/2 C tahini paste (100% whole sesame)
- + juice of 1 lemon
- 1 TSP cumin powder
- 1 clove of garlic
- 1/2 C cooking water (or more)

for serving:

- + sweet paprika
- + olive oil
- + chopped parsley

Hummus is probably one of the most popular dishes in our house. There is nothing like homemade hummus. The freshness and the flavor are unbeatable! It's loaded with fiber for digestion and antioxidants that help regulate blood sugar and decrease cardiovascular risks.

Check out my tip on how to soak and cook beans (page 218).

In a food processor, add 2/3 of the cooked garbanzo beans, leave 1/3 aside for garnish.

Blend all ingredients in a food processor until smooth and creamy. If needed, add more water.

Garnish with the garbanzo beans that you kept aside, chopped parsley, sweet paprika and extra virgin olive oil.

Serve slightly warm with pita bread.

4-6 *servings*

 GF

for the lentils:

1 C   black lentils
1 C   water

for the dip:

1/2 C   water (use the water the
          lentils were cooked in)
1 C   tahini paste
  +   salt
  +   pepper

BLACK LENTIL DIP

Hummus can be made in so many ways with so many different ingredients! I did a spin on the traditional hummus by using black lentils and tahini. The flavor is so delicious! Plus, this hummus is great for entertaining. Yummy on a sandwich, as an appetizer, on a crunchy baguette, your favorite cracker, or getting your kids to eat veggies.

In a saucepan, add lentils, water and salt. Cook until tender. Save 1/2 cup of the water when straining the lentils.

In a food processor, add the water, drained lentils, tahini, salt and pepper. Blend until completely smooth. Pour into a serving bowl.

Enjoy with your favorite crackers or veggies.

Yield

6-8 *servings*

 GF

1 C   raw slivered almonds, soaked overnight and drained
1   clove of garlic
+   juice of 1 lemon
2 TBSP   olive oil
1/4 C   water
+   salt
+   pepper

ALMOND FETA CHEESE

Great alternative for feta cheese, only much healthier and better tasting. Your kids won't even notice the difference.

This cheese can also be used to form a hard, sliceable cheese. Simply place the cheese in a cheesecloth in a container in the fridge to drain the liquids overnight. Remove the cheesecloth, place on a baking sheet, and then bake at 375° F for 20-30 minutes until the top becomes golden-brown. Let cool, and slice to serve.

In a food processor, add all ingredients and blend until you reach a feta cheese consistency. From time to time, stop and scrape the sides.

Serve on a fresh baguette or with your favorite veggies.

Sprinkle with some pepper, and if you wish, some more olive oil for extra flavor and deliciousness!

Yield

12-15 *cheese balls*

 GF

1 C	raw cashew, soaked 2-3 hours and drained
1 TBSP	gf white miso paste
1 TBSP	nutritional yeast
1/2 TSP	mustard
2 TBSP	olive oil
1 TBSP	lemon juice
1 TSP	onion powder
1/2 TSP	sweet paprika
2 TBSP	water
+	salt
+	pepper

topping:

+ toasted sesame seeds
+ nigella seeds

These cheese balls are great for entertaining. They look pretty, taste delicious and are a wonderful substitute for cheese. They are also excellent as a spread on a sandwich or your favorite cracker.

It is also a good substitute for "white sauce" on pasta. So many things you can do with this recipe. Be creative.

CASHEW CHEESE BALLS

In a food processor, add all ingredients and blend to a paste-like consistency.

Wet your hands and form the mixture into balls or use a small ice cream scoop, dipped in water to prevent from sticking.

Pour sesame seeds into one bowl. Pour nigella seeds into another bowl. Roll and completely cover half of the balls in sesame seeds and the other half in nigella seeds

Serve with your favorite crackers and veggies. Or skip the step of forming the balls and serve in a bowl.

Yield

4-6 *servings*

1 C   raw cashews, soaked
        overnight and drained
1/2 TSP   salt
1 TSP   agave
2 TBSP   chopped onion
2 TBSP   lemon juice
1/3 C   water

for serving:

+   nigella seeds
+   diced tomatoes

CREAMY CASHEW SPREAD

I was never a fan of eating meat, but I was definitely a cheese lover, so I'm trying to find alternatives that are good for my body and my health.

This creamy cashew spread is a great alternative to a picante-type cheese. The onions make it unique and creamy. I let my daughter (my biggest critic) try some, and she loved it! The flavors blend perfectly with tomatoes and nigella seeds.

Add all ingredients into a food processor and blend for a few minutes, scraping the sides from time to time until you reach a creamy texture.

Spread on slice of bread, top with diced tomatoes, sprinkle some nigella seeds, and serve.

1   eggplant
1/4 C tahini paste
1 TBSP date syrup
  +   salt
  +   pepper

ROASTED EGGPLANT WITH TAHINI & DATE SYRUP

Roasted eggplant can be made in so many ways. From traditional recipes with oil and garlic to Balkanic ones with mayo and salt, there are dozens of possibilities. I really like this recipe because it combines salty and sweet. It brings out a unique flavor that is decadent and gourmet.

Preheat oven to broil.

Take a baking sheet and place the eggplant on it. With a knife, make several slits in the eggplant. Put the baking sheet on the middle rack of the oven. Roast on each side for about 20-25 minutes, until completely soft. Let the eggplant cool. Then, cut the eggplant in half, lengthwise, and scrape out the flesh into a strainer to drain the excess liquid.

In a mixing bowl, add tahini, date syrup, salt and pepper. Mix well.

Add the eggplant and mix.

Serve with crackers or as a spread on toast.

Yield

4-6 *servings*

1 TSP	olive oil
1	large onion, chopped
2	cloves garlic, minced
5	organic zucchinis, cut into cubes
1 TBSP	hemp seeds
1/2 C	raw walnuts
+	salt
+	pepper

ZUCCHINI SPREAD

Zucchini spread is one of my favorite snacks. It is low in calories, loaded with fiber and can lower your blood sugar. It's also great for the digestive system.

This zucchini spread is decadent, smooth, nutty, and goes so well with my homemade gluten-free crackers (page 53). It is also good with fresh bell peppers, cucumbers and celery sticks.

In a nonstick pan, add olive oil, onion, salt and pepper. Sauté for a few minutes then add garlic and zucchini. Continue to sauté until completely tender and the liquids have evaporated.

In a food processor, add the zucchini mixture, hemp seeds, walnuts, and a tad more salt and pepper. Blend until smooth.

Serve warm or cold with your favorite veggies or crackers.

6-8 *servings*

2 C   onions, chopped
2 TBSP   olive oil, divided
1 C   dried black beans or red
kidney beans, soaked
overnight, cooked and
drained
1/3 C   raw walnuts
1 TBSP   cognac
+   salt
+   pepper

Growing up in a Jewish home means eating chopped liver during every holiday.

The taste of chopped liver is very distinct. The main ingredient besides liver is onion, which gives it its signature flavor. You will not believe how easy it is to make a vegan alternative to chopped liver.

The version that I'm making is a pâté and has no aftertaste versus eating real liver. The crunchiness from the walnuts along with the sweetness of the sautéed onions and the creaminess of the beans produces a perfect and delicious vegan pâté. It is so much better for your body than real liver and it's packed with proteins and vitamins.

Check out my tip on how to soak and cook beans (page 218).

VEGAN PÂTÉ

In a nonstick pan, add one tablespoon olive oil, onions, salt and pepper. Sauté until tender.

Pour sautéed onions and cooked beans into a food processor, add walnuts, another tablespoon olive oil, and cognac. Pulse to a pâté-like consistency.

Spread on a cracker or toast and serve at room temperature.

PUFF PASTRY BUREK FILLED WITH FETA CHEESE & OLIVES

Yield

10-12 *bureks*

almond feta cheese:

1 C	raw slivered almonds, soaked overnight and drained
1	clove of garlic
+	juice of 1 lemon
2 TBSP	olive oil
1/4 C	water
+	salt
+	pepper

burek pastry:

8 OZ	vegan puff pastry, 1 roll
5	black olives, pitted
+	olive oil to brush the burek
+	raw sesame seeds

Heat oven to 400° F.

almond feta cheese:

In a food processor, add all the cheese ingredients and blend for a few minutes. From time to time, stop and scrape the sides. Process until creamy.

burek pastry:

Thaw the puff pastry in the fridge overnight.

In a food processor, add the cheese and olives. Pulse until blended.

Roll the pastry dough into a thin sheet. Spread the olive cheese evenly onto the dough. Then roll the dough into a roulade. Slice the roulade into 3/4" pieces.

Line a baking sheet with parchment paper. Lay the bureks on the parchment paper, brush with olive oil, sprinkle with sesame seeds and bake for about 30 minutes. Serve warm or at room temperature.

We use raw slivered almonds without the shell so that our cheese will turn white.

One of the most common snacks in Israel is burek. You can find burek in every supermarket's bakery section. They come with all sorts of fillings—cheese, mushrooms, spinach, feta, olives, mashed potatoes and more. The smells that filled my childhood are hard to convey, but the aroma of these bureks baking comes very close.

I remember going with my mom to the supermarket and she would always treat me to my favorite burek, a cheese-filled one. I created a vegan cheese burek but took it up a notch by adding olives. I just love the flakiness of bureks with the creaminess of the cheese inside. It doesn't get much better than that. Not a low calorie snack but a delicious one for sure.

Yield

4-6 *servings*

 GF

+ seasoned seaweed (0.2 oz/6 g)
1/2 C vegan mayonnaise
1 TBSP mustard
3 C garbanzo beans, soaked overnight, cooked and drained (measurement refers to the cooked beans)
3 green onions, chopped
1/2 red bell pepper, chopped
1 clove of garlic, minced
1 jalapeño, chopped (without seeds)
2 celery stalks, chopped
+ salt
+ pepper

This is a winning recipe! If you are tired of boring lunch sandwiches, you'll love this super easy and super flavorful recipe. What a great protein-packed spread that truly tastes like real tuna salad—only so much better (and without tuna's aftertaste and smell).

Check out my tip on how to soak and cook beans (page 218).

MOCK TUNA SALAD

In a food processor, add seaweed and pulse a few times until it becomes a sand-like texture.

Add mayo and mustard and pulse a couple more times.

Add the garbanzo beans and pulse about 3-4 times, but not too much or it will lose its tuna-like texture.

Add chopped onions, pepper, garlic, jalapeño, celery, salt and pepper. Pulse a couple of times, just enough to combine the ingredients.

Spread on your favorite bread.

Keep in an air tight container in the fridge for up to 5 days.

1	package of frozen artichoke hearts (8 oz/226 g), thawed
3/4 C	gf bread crumbs
2 TBSP	nutritional yeast
3	green onions, chopped
1 TBSP	olive oil
+	salt
+	pepper
+	olive oil spray

Stuffed artichoke hearts add elegance to a meal. They're great as an appetizer and easy to make. This dish has a delicate flavor and a lovely texture— crunchy on the outside and soft on the inside.

STUFFED ARTICHOKE HEARTS

Heat oven to 375° F.

Line a baking sheet with parchment paper.

In a mixing bowl, add bread crumbs, nutritional yeast, green onions, salt, pepper and olive oil. Mix well.

Press a spoonful of the filling firmly into each artichoke heart. Place the stuffed artichokes on the baking sheet. Spray the top with olive oil and bake for about 15 minutes, until the bread crumbs are golden brown.

Yield

6-8 *servings*

 GF

3 C   carrots
1   package sun dried tomatoes (3.5 oz/100 g)
1 1/2 C   roasted buckwheat
1 C   flaxseed meal
1 C   roasted chestnuts
1 TSP   garam masala
1 TSP   chili powder
1/2 C   olive oil
1 TBSP   lemon juice
+   salt
+   pepper

dipping sauce:

1   can diced tomatoes (14.5 oz/411 g)
1   can roasted red peppers (7.75 oz/220 g)
+   salt
+   pepper
2 TSP   pure maple syrup
1 TBSP   vegetable base
2 TBSP   water

With the dipping sauce or without, it's up to you. Great for a party, for dinner, over couscous, or any other occasion—you decide.

COCKTAIL MEAT(LESS) BALLS

Heat oven to 375° F.

Prepare a baking sheet with parchment paper.

In a food processor, add carrots, sun dried tomatoes, buckwheat, flaxseed meal, chestnut, garam masala and chili powder.

Pulse and scrape the sides until blended but not smooth. Then add olive oil, lemon juice, salt and pepper while simultaneously pulsing.

Using a small ice cream scoop, create evenly sized balls. (Wet the scoop and your hands with warm water to prevent sticking.) Bake in the oven for about 15-20 minutes.

dipping sauce:

Mix all the ingredients in a food processor.

Pour into a sauce pan and warm through. Serve.

Yield

4-6 *servings*

1 1/2 C   organic sprouted spelt
         flour
1 1/2 C   unbleached white flour
1 TBSP   baking powder
1 TSP   salt
1   bottle of lager beer (11.2
      oz / 330 ml)

topping:

1 TBSP   olive oil
1 TBSP   flax seeds

BEER BREAD

This is my go-to bread. It's so easy to make and tastes delicious without the added preservatives and chemicals of a store bought bread. You can add olives, nuts and whatever spices or seeds you like to the batter. Be creative.

Heat oven to 375° F.

Add the flours, baking powder and salt to a food processor, pulse twice, then add the beer gently. Start pulsing until combined.

Take a loaf pan and spray with olive oil. Pour the dough into the pan. Brush with olive oil and sprinkle with flax seeds. Bake for about 30 minutes, until a toothpick comes out dry.

You can modify the topping with your favorite grains such as sesame seeds and/or sunflower seeds.

Yield

1 C   *parmesan*

1 C   raw cashews
1/4 C   nutritional yeast
1 1/2 TSP   salt

CHEESE-FREE PARMESAN

Use this cheese-free Parmesan as a topping on your favorite steamed vegetables or pasta.

In a food processor, add cashews, nutritional yeast and salt.

Pulse until the texture becomes fine like sand.

Keep in an air tight container in the fridge.

Yield

4-6 *servings*

1   bag of frozen cut okra
    (16 oz/454 g)
1 TBSP   olive oil
1 C   gf panko bread crumbs
  +   salt
  +   pepper
1 TSP   sweet paprika
1 TSP   garlic powder
  +   olive oil spray

BAKED OKRA

Okra is one of my favorite vegetables. Not only does it have numerous healthy ingredients like fiber, which is good for cholesterol management, but it also contains folic acid, vitamin B and vitamin A. It is low in calories and has one of the highest levels of antioxidants found in a green vegetable. Okra is also a good source of important minerals such as iron, calcium and magnesium.

Great as a snack, side dish, or appetizer.

Heat oven to 375° F.

Defrost the okra and strain excess water.

Line a baking sheet with parchment paper.

Place bread crumbs in one bowl.

In another bowl, add the thawed okra and drizzle with olive oil. Add salt, pepper, paprika and garlic powder. Mix well.

Roll the okra pods in the bread crumbs, covering all sides. Place the okra on the baking sheet. Spray with olive oil and bake until golden brown, about 20 minutes.

Yield

4-6 *servings*

6-7 small yams, washed and cut into strips
2 TBSP olive oil
+ salt
+ pepper
+ sweet paprika

BAKED YAM FRIES

Yams are so delicious! Sweet and salty, satisfying, and much healthier than regular potato fries.

They are loaded with fiber, potassium, vitamin A and vitamin C, which helps keep your immune system strong. Yams are also a good source of antioxidants, which lower cholesterol and keep your heart healthy.

You can enjoy yams as a side dish, snack or even a yummy appetizer along with a spicy dip.

Heat oven to 375° F.

Line a baking sheet with parchment paper.

In a mixing bowl, add the yams, olive oil, salt, pepper and sweet paprika. Mix well.

Lay the yams on the baking sheet in one layer and bake for about 30 minutes until tender and golden brown.

Yield

6-8 *servings*

 (GF)

falafel:

2	cloves garlic
4 C	cooked garbanzo beans
4 C	fresh parsley
1	medium onion, cubed
1 TBSP	cumin
1 TSP	baking powder
1 TSP	turmeric
1 TSP	Old Bay Seasoning
2 TBSP	olive oil
✦	salt
✦	pepper
✦	olive oil spray

*tahini sauce
(optional topping):*

1 C	tahini paste
3/4 C	lukewarm water
1	clove garlic
✦	juice of 1 lemon
✦	bunch of fresh parsley
✦	salt

For those who like falafel but not the extra calories, this is a great, lighter version.

This baked falafel recipe doesn't compromise taste. It is not as crispy as fried falafel, but when served in a whole wheat pita with tahini and tomatoes, it sure matches the flavor.

Check out my tip on how to soak and cook beans (page 218).

BAKED FALAFEL

falafel:

Heat oven to 375° F.

Line a baking sheet with parchment paper.

In a food processor, add all ingredients and pulse to mix coarsely, or smoothly if you prefer.

Using a small ice cream scoop, form evenly sized falafel balls and place on baking sheet. Spray the tops with olive oil and bake for about 15-20 minutes.

Serve over a thick slice of tomato and drizzle with tahini sauce.

tahini sauce (optional topping):

In a food processor, add all of the ingredients. Mix until smooth and serve.

Yield

1   *jar*

 GF

1	package dried chili pods (8 oz/226.7 g)
2	heads garlic, peeled
1/4 C	coconut oil
1/2 C	olive oil or more
1 TBSP	turmeric powder
1 TBSP	cumin powder
1 TBSP	salt

This is a great base that you can keep in a mason jar in the fridge and use for so many dishes.

It is loaded with flavor, good oils, and warm spices. The smell is so fragrant. You can use it as a base for a rice dish, soup, chili, stew, or anything else you can think of. The great thing about it is that you are in control of what you put into it, which means healthy ingredients and no artificial flavors or preservatives.

HOMEMADE CHILI GARLIC BASE

Remove stem and chop chili pods into manageable pieces. In a coffee ginder, grind small batches of the chopped chili pods into a powder.

In a food processor, add chili powder, garlic, coconut oil, olive oil, turmeric, cumin and salt. Mix until it becomes a paste.

Keep in a mason jar in the refrigerator.

6-8 *servings*

 GF

pink tahini:

1	beet, peeled and steamed
1 C	tahini paste
2 TBSP	fresh lemon juice
1 C	water
+	salt
+	pepper

roasted eggplant:

4	eggplants
+	olive oil
+	salt

for serving:

| + | garnish with roasted pine nuts. |

Pink tahini over roasted eggplant is not only a colorful dish, but is also super healthy, nutritious and delicious. The crunch from the pine nuts, the softness of the eggplant, along with the tang of the lemony beet tahini create a yummy, sophisticated dish, full of interesting flavors and colors.

PINK TAHINI OVER ROASTED EGGPLANT

pink tahini:

In a food processor, add all the ingredients and blend until very smooth. Set aside.

roasted eggplant:

Heat oven to 375° F.

Cut the eggplants in half lengthwise. Use a knife to cut criss-cross slits on the flesh part. Drizzle with olive oil, salt and pepper. Take a baking sheet lined with parchment paper and lay the eggplants on it face down.

Bake for 45 minutes, until very tender.

assembly:

Lay the egglplant facing up on a serving plate. Drizzle with pink tahini, sprinkle with pine nuts and parsley. Serve warm.

Yield

4-6 *servings*

1 TSP	olive oil
1	clove of garlic, minced
1	package of frozen and thawed okra (16 oz/454 g)
1	can tomato sauce (15 oz/425 g)
1 1/2 TSP	pure maple syrup
+	salt
+	pepper

OKRA IN RED SAUCE

Okra is a superfood that has very few calories, is low in fat and rich in vitamins, minerals and fiber. It is also known for having high amounts of antioxidants.

Eating healthy doesn't mean eating food that isn't tasty. If you make it right, healthy food can definitely be tasty.

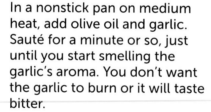

In a nonstick pan on medium heat, add olive oil and garlic. Sauté for a minute or so, just until you start smelling the garlic's aroma. You don't want the garlic to burn or it will taste bitter.

Add the tomato sauce, salt pepper and pure maple syrup. Continue to cook for 2 minutes over medium heat.

Add okra. Lower heat and let simmer for about 30 minutes, until it's soft but not mushy.

Yield

4-6 *servings*

1   roll of puff pastry,
      thawed (8 oz/227 g)
1 TBSP olive oil
1 TBSP nigella seeds
2 LB   asparagus
      (about 26-30 stalks)

ASPARAGUS WRAPPED IN PUFF PASTRY

What better appetizer than asparagus puff pastry? Veggies with some carbs will satisfy a craving in no time. Not an entirely guilt-free choice, but not the worst one either. Serve plain or with a dipping sauce. It is a beautiful dish that never fails to impress. Most importantly, everyone is able to make it—no need to be a chef.

Heat oven to 375° F.

Line a baking sheet with parchment paper.

Trim the asparagus to your liking.

Bring a steam pot of water to a boil. Add the asparagus with heads up. Steam for 2 minutes and gently strain. Set aside.

In the meantime, flatten the dough with a rolling pin. Cut long thin strips, about 1/4" wide. Wrap one strip of dough around each individual asparagus stalk in an upwards spiral, and place on baking sheet.

Use a silicone brush to brush the top of the pastries with olive oil.

Sprinkle with nigella seeds and bake for about 20 minutes. Serve warm.

Yield

6-8 *servings*

2 C	chickpeas, soaked overnight, cooked and drained or canned and drained
2 TBSP	extra virgin olive oil
1/2 TSP	smoked paprika
1/4 TSP	cumin
1/4 TSP	kosher salt
2 C	pinto beans, soaked overnight, cooked and drained or canned and drained
2 TBSP	extra virgin olive oil
1/2 TSP	smoked paprika
1/2 TSP	cumin
1/4 TSP	kosher salt

Roast your own chickpeas and beans to get your crunchy fix without compromising quality or nutritional values. Be in charge of the salt and spices you use. Plus, then you know there are no preservatives of any kind in your beans.

When you roast your own beans, they won't last long. The minute they are out of the oven, all crunchy and spicy, your family will snack on them until they're gone.

I always use a good quality extra virgin olive oil to get the best flavor possible.

Check out my tip on how to soak and cook beans (page 218).

ROASTED CHICKPEAS & ROASTED PINTO BEANS

Heat oven to 400° F.

In a bowl, mix the chickpeas with the first list of spices with your hands until fully coated.

In another bowl, mix the pinto beans with the second list of spices, until fully coated.

Line a baking sheet with parchment paper. Spread the chickpeas evenly and flat on a single layer. Do the same with the pinto beans on a separate baking sheet.

Bake in the oven for about 30 minutes.

Let cool and serve.

Yield

4-6 *servings*

3 C pinto beans, soaked overnight, cooked and drained (measurement refers to the cooked beans)

2 green onions, chopped

14 kalamata olives, pitted and sliced

2 TBSP olive oil

+ salt

+ pepper

The new hit in my house is this delicious bean salad. My daughter, my husband and I are addicted.

So good, so simple, and who would have thought that a combination of olives and beans could be so good?

Adding green onion helps the flavors marry and ties the whole dish together.

I just love the simplicity of this recipe. I like to eat this bean salad on a bed of kale and sliced tomatoes, giving me a balanced meal that is so satisfying. By the way, you can use any beans you like. I tried the salad with lima beans and it was delicious and creamy. However, lima beans don't keep their shape as well as pinto beans, so if serving guests, remember pinto beans will look more appealing.

Check out my tip on how to soak and cook beans (page 218).

PINTO BEAN SALAD

Mix the beans, green onion and olives.

Drizzle with olive oil, salt and pepper.

Mix and serve.

Yield

4-6 *servings*

(GF)

2 C gf whole grain oat flour
      or gf flour blend
1/2 C water
1/2 C olive oil
1 TBSP nigella seeds
2 TBSP sunflower seeds
+ salt

I make these crackers with gluten-free whole grain oat flour, but if you are not allergic to gluten, you can certainly use your favorite flour instead. These gourmet crackers turn out crunchy, flavorful, and elegant. The nigella and sunflower seeds add so much flavor, they make the cracker.

Nigella seeds, also called black cumin seeds, are known for their endless health benefits! I am trying to avoid processed food as much as possible. If you read the labels on a typical bag of crackers you buy at the store, you won't believe how long the list of ingredients is, including harmful preservatives and toxins. When you make your own crackers, you take control of the amount of sodium and the quality of the ingredients you use.

These crackers melt in your mouth, and the only downside is that they disappear way too quickly.

OAT CRACKERS

Heat oven to 350° F.

Line two large baking sheets with parchment paper.

In a mixer with a dough hook, add flour and salt. Then add water and oil, and work the dough until nice and firm.

Dust a wooden dough roller with flour.

Cut the dough in half. On the parchment paper, roll each half into a thin layer, but not so thin it breaks apart.

Sprinkle with nigella and sunflower seeds. Press the seeds into the dough with the roller. Then cut lines into the dough with a sharp knife, making a grid of squares.

Bake for 15-20 minutes. Let cool and break along the cuts.

Enjoy with your favorite spread.

Yield

12 *bites*

GF

2	8 oz packages vegan herb & chives cream cheese
1 C	gf flour blend
1 TSP	baking powder
1 TBSP	olive oil
+	salt
+	pepper

topping:

+ nigella seeds

CHEESY BITES

Cheesy bites are an amazing complement to any wintery soup. It is so wonderful that just a few ingredients can create these lovely, crunchy bites.

Heat oven to 375°.

In a mixing bowl or food processor, mix all the ingredients to a smooth and even texture.

Spray a mini muffin pan with olive oil. Divide the dough into about 12 evenly sized bites and sprinkle with nigella seeds. Cook for about 20-30 minutes until golden brown.

Yield

4-6 *servings*

3 C   cherry heirloom
       tomatoes, halved
1 C   yellow and red peppers,
       cubed
1/2 C   cilantro, chopped
1/2 C   parsley, chopped

dressing:

1 TBSP   olive oil
1 TSP   balsamic vinegar
   ✛   juice of 1/2 lemon
   ✛   salt
   ✛   pepper

TOMATOES, PEPPERS CILANTRO & PARSLEY

It's never too boring to eat a tomato salad, especially when you know that it's loaded with so many vitamins and nutrients—vitamin C, antioxidants, iron and many more. But even if you ignore all the health benefits, you can't get away from the amazing flavor and freshness of this salad.

Use heirloom tomatoes to take it up a notch! Good balsamic and quality olive oil are key. Just a few ingredients go a long way. Less is definitely more with this salad.

Mix all salad ingredients in a bowl.

Mix all dressing ingredients in another bowl.

Pour the dressing over the salad and serve.

Yield

4-6 *servings*

2 1/2 C fresh green chickpeas, cooked and divided (you can find them in the freezer section)
1/3 C tahini paste
1/3 C greek pepperoncinis
2/3 C water
1 TBSP olive oil
  + juice of 1/2 lemon
  + lemon
  + pepper

Fresh green chickpeas are a big deal for me. I could not believe I found them in the freezer section at the supermarket the other day. I had never worked with fresh chickpeas before, so I was excited to see what I could come up with using them in the kitchen.

Normally I like to add them to salads, but the expert hummus-maker in me thought why not create a spread out of them. Sure enough, I tried and it turned out amazing. Super simple to make and a great protein source. I even use it as a spread in my kids' lunches. Top it with celery, lettuce, tomatoes, avocado, and any other vegetable you prefer. It's so good.

FRESH GREEN CHICKPEA SPREAD

In a food processor, add 2 cups chickpeas (set aside the other 1/2 cup), tahini, pepperoncinis, water, olive oil, lemon, salt and pepper. Blend until smooth.

Add the 1/2 cup cooked chickpeas to the mixture and mix in using a spatula.

Spread on your favorite bread or cracker. Top with thinly sliced celery, a sprinkle of pink Himalayan salt, pepper and a drizzle of olive oil. Enjoy!

Yield

6 *servings*

1 C	quinoa
1 1/2 C	water
1/2 TSP	salt
1 TBSP	olive oil
1	onion, chopped
2	cloves garlic, minced
4	celery stalks, chopped
1 C	carrots, chopped
1 TSP	turmeric
+	salt
+	pepper

QUINOA PILAF

Quinoa pilaf is a great vegan meal option. It is a wonderful way to recreate a classic rice pilaf dish. The quinoa brings out a unique flavor that's a bit more nutty than rice. Quinoa is considered a super food protein and is gluten-free, high in magnesium, iron and calcium.

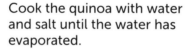

Cook the quinoa with water and salt until the water has evaporated.

In a nonstick pan, add olive oil, onion, garlic and celery. Sauté until tender.

Add carrots, salt and pepper. Sauté for a few more minutes.

Add turmeric. Sauté for a couple more minutes.

Add the cooked quinoa and mix until the flavors are evenly distributed. Serve warm.

6-8 *servings*

 GF

2 TBSP	olive oil, divided
1	small onion, chopped
3-4	cloves garlic, minced
2 TBSP	sweet paprika
1 TSP	turmeric
1 TSP	cumin
5	green onions, chopped
1 TSP	dried cilantro
1/8 TSP	cayenne pepper
1/8 TSP	pepper flakes
3 C	water
4 C	dried chickpeas, soaked overnight and drained
+	salt
+	pepper

garnish:

+ handful of parsley or cilantro, chopped

Chickpeas are a very important component in a vegan diet. They provide protein and other nutrition that your body needs on a daily basis. A diet that is rich in protein is much needed since the absorption of protein from a plant-based diet is lower than that of an animal-product-based diet. Therefore, we need to consume more protein to maintain healthy levels of it in the body. This dish is very good as a side dish or as a main dish on top of brown rice. Chickpeas are great for diabetics since they have a low glycemic index. Also, regular intake of chickpeas can lower your cholesterol levels and therefore are good for your heart.

MOROCCAN CHICKPEAS

Heat stove to medium heat.

In a cast iron pot, heat 1 tablespoon olive oil. Add onion, salt and pepper. Sauté for a couple of minutes.

Add garlic and sauté for a few more minutes.

Begin adding the spices. Start with paprika, turmeric and cumin. Add another tablespoon olive oil and let the spices sizzle for a minute or two.

Then slowly add water (about 1 cup). Bring to a boil. Add the green onions, cilantro, cayenne pepper, pepper flakes, and more salt and pepper. Stir.

Add the chickpeas and the rest of the water. Lower the heat to low and cook for about 45 minutes.

Let sit for 15 minutes before serving.

Garnish with parsley or cilantro and serve.

To learn more about how to soak and cook beans, see tip (page 218).

CHALLAH BREAD

Yield

1-2 *loaves*

1	package dry yeast (1/4 oz/7 g)
1 C	lukewarm water
2 TBSP	agave
1/4 C	olive oil
1 1/2 TSP	kosher salt
4 C	unbleached all purpose organic flour

topping:

+ sesame seeds

In a mixing bowl, dissolve yeast in lukewarm water. Let bubble for about 10-15 minutes.

Add agave, olive oil and salt.

Start adding flour one cup at a time while the mixer is on a low setting using a dough hook. Continue until all the flour has been added and the dough is formed. If it's too sticky, add a little more flour.

Place the dough in a mixing bowl dusted with flour. Cover with plastic wrap and lay a clean towel on top. Let rise for a couple of hours, until it doubles in size.

Heat the oven to 375° F.

Knead the rising dough to remove any air. Divide the dough into three equal pieces.

Roll the dough into strands of equal length. Braid the three strands and when finished, connect the two ends, seam side down, so it forms a circle—just like I did in the picture.

Let it rise for about 1/2 hour to 1 hour.

Brush the top with olive oil and sprinkle with sesame seeds. Bake in the oven for about 25-30 minutes.

———————— ————————

There is nothing like the smell of fresh baked challah. Usually on Friday I bake it for Shabbat dinner. It's something for my family to look forward to. It may sound difficult to bake challah, but it's actually so easy. I like to shape it into a circle for a festive and elegant look. Or be creative and make your own unique shape.

———————— ✿ ————————

Free for all ages! Is your life too plastic?

Watch the fun, informative, spirited, *short* documentary film *Bag-It* about one man's journey to lead a plastic bag free life. Learn about plastic pollution and what you can do about it. Hear about the effort to pass a **Reusable Bag Ordinance** in Everett.

Presented in partnership with 350 Everett
and Zero Waste Washington.

Location: **Our Saviors Lutheran Church**
215 W. Mukilteo Blvd, Everett

Doors open 6:30 pm, film starts at **7:00 pm**

Cost: Free and includes popcorn!

Questions: Contact Pam at EverettRBO@gmail.com

SOUPS
& *Salads*

Yield

4-6 *servings*

1 TSP	olive oil
1	onion, chopped
3	celery stalks, chopped
1	parsnip, peeled and chopped
3	carrots, chopped
1	red bell pepper, chopped
1/2 C	pearl barley
6 C	water
1	can organic tomato sauce 15 oz/425 g
1 TSP	turmeric
1/2 TSP	agave
1 TSP	no chicken base
1 TSP	no beef base
3 TBSP	dried parsley
1 TSP	cumin
1 C	fresh cilantro, chopped
+	salt
+	pepper

COUNTRY-STYLE SOUP

When my parents visit for the holidays, for them, a meal is not complete without soup. They prefer vegetable soup, so I created this soup using warm spices and root vegetables. The outcome was a hearty, flavorful, and rich soup.

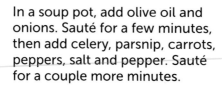

In a soup pot, add olive oil and onions. Sauté for a few minutes, then add celery, parsnip, carrots, peppers, salt and pepper. Sauté for a couple more minutes.

Add pearl barley. Sauté for one minute. Add water, tomato sauce, turmeric, agave, no chicken base, no beef base, parsley and cumin. Bring to a boil, then lower to simmer and cook for about 30 minutes.

Garnish with cilantro and serve.

Yield

6-8 *servings*

1 TBSP olive oil
2 large leeks, sliced and washed
1 TSP fresh ginger, grated
1 TSP turmeric
5-6 C butternut squash, roasted and puréed
7 C water
+ salt
+ pepper
+ sunflower seeds for garnish

A quick recipe that every beginner can handle. Very satisfying, sweet and salty, and super yummy. Great for a Thanksgiving dinner!

Leeks always carry dirt, therefore, they need to be soaked. You want to slice into rings first, then separate and place into a large bowl of water. Next, dry in a salad spinner or with a clean towel.

ROASTED BUTTERNUT SQUASH & GINGER SOUP

In a cast iron pot, add olive oil and leeks. Sauté until tender,

Add salt, pepper, ginger and turmeric. Cook until the spices become fragrant.

Add the roasted butternut squash purée, water, salt and pepper.

Bring to a boil then reduce to a simmer for a few minutes to let the flavors combine.

Using a hand blender, blend until silky smooth.

Garnish with sunflower seeds and serve.

Yield

6-8 *servings*

black beans:

2 C dried black beans
4 C water
  + salt

soup:

1 TBSP olive oil
  1 medium onion, chopped
  2 cloves garlic, minced
  7 medium size golden
     potatoes, peeled and
     cubed
  4 C water
  + salt
  + pepper

topping:

  + olive oil

Less is definitely more in this soup. The simplicity of the ingredients are key.

CREAMY POTATO SOUP TOPPED WITH BLACK BEANS

black beans:

Soak 2 cups of black beans in water overnight (refer to page 218 for tips on soaking beans).

Cook the beans in salty water until tender. Drain and set aside.

soup:

In a cast iron pot on medium heat, add olive oil and onion. Sauté for a couple of minutes until translucent. Add garlic and cook for another minute.

Add potatoes, salt and pepper. Sauté for a couple of minutes.

Add water and bring to a boil. Lower the heat and let cook until the potatoes are completely softened.

Blend the soup with a hand blender until creamy and smooth. If you wish, add more olive oil.

Top the soup with the black beans, drizzle with some olive oil and serve.

Yield

6-8 *servings*

pearl barley:

1 C	pearl barley
2 C	water
+	salt

soup:

1 TBSP	olive oil
1	medium onion, chopped
2	shallots, chopped
1	clove of garlic, minced
1 TBSP	chopped fresh ginger
6	organic zucchinis, cubed
5 C	water
1 TBSP	vegetable base
1	bunch of fresh cilantro
+	salt
+	pepper

topping:

+	olive oil

Creamy zucchini soup is so divine. The combination of the zucchini's smooth texture with the crunchiness of the pearl barley, along with onion and cilantro, delivers a whole meal. It is satisfying and easy to make. Serve in a mug with a fresh sliced baguette and vegan almond feta cheese (page 31).

Tip: replace the pearl barley with brown rice for a GF soup.

ZUCCHINI & PEARL BARLEY SOUP

pearl barley:

In a saucepan on medium heat, add pearl barley, water, salt and pepper. Cook until all water has been absorbed. Set aside.

soup:

In a cast iron soup pot on medium heat, add olive oil, onions, shallots, and garlic. Sauté until the onions are tender.

Add ginger. Sauté for one minute.

Add zucchinis, water, and vegetable base. Cook until zucchini is soft.

Add cilantro and cook for 5 more minutes.

Blend the soup with a hand blender until creamy.

Pour the cooked pearl barley into the zucchini soup.

Drizzle with olive oil and serve.

6-8 *servings*

1 TSP   olive oil
1   onion, thinly chopped
2   cloves garlic, minced
1   parsnip, grated
2 C   roasted chestnuts, ground in a coffee grinder or in a food processor
3 C   organic frozen corn, thawed
4 C   water
1 TBSP   gf light soy sauce/tamari
1   can light coconut milk, 14 oz/400 ml
+   salt
+   pepper

CORN, CHESTNUT & COCONUT SOUP

Winter is the perfect time to eat a nice hearty soup. I roasted the chestnuts myself, but you can choose to buy the prepackaged ones as well.

In a cast iron pot on medium-high heat, add olive oil, chopped onion, garlic, salt and pepper. Sauté until tender.

Add parsnip and chestnuts. Sauté for a couple more minutes.

Add corn, water and soy sauce. Bring to a boil then lower heat to a simmer and cook for about 20 minutes. Add coconut milk. Cook for 10 more minutes and serve.

4-6 *servings*

1 TSP	olive oil
1	medium onion, chopped
1	clove garlic, minced
3 C	fresh white beans
3 C	boiling water
2 TBSP	tomato paste
1 TSP	sweet paprika
1 TBSP	molasses
1	bay leaf
+	salt
+	pepper

COOKED FRESH BEANS

I recently saw fresh beans for the first time at a local farm. I had taken my kids to a pumpkin patch and while they ran around in the corn maze, I checked out the local produce. I saw these beautiful pods with white and purple tie-dye-like lines. So pretty. I got so excited and immediately filled up a bag and cooked up this yummy dish.

Highly recommended. If you ever have the chance to buy fresh produce in season, do it. The flavors are absolutely amazing.

In a pot on medium heat, add olive oil and sauté onions and garlic until tender.

Add the beans and remaining ingredients.

Bring to a boil then reduce to a simmer for about 1 hour, until the beans are soft and the sauce has thickened.

Yield

6-8 *servings*

 GF

1 TBSP   olive oil
1   large onion, chopped
1   clove garlic, minced
4 C   chanterelle mushrooms, thinly sliced
1   rutabaga, peeled and cut into small cubes
1 TBSP   no chicken base
6 C   water
1/3 C   red wine
1/3 C   fresh parsley
1/3 C   coconut water
+   salt
+   pepper

CHANTERELLE MUSHROOMS & RUTABAGA SOUP

Chanterelle mushrooms are so delicious no matter what the method of cooking. Roasted, in a soup or casserole, you name it.

Chanterelle mushrooms are a great source of protein, copper, potassium, zinc, selenium and B vitamins. They're low in fat and high in fiber.

This creamy yet figure-friendly soup is light in calories but loaded with flavor, and more importantly, easy to make.

In a heavy cast iron pot on medium heat, add olive oil, onion, garlic, salt and pepper. Sauté for a couple of minutes.

Add mushrooms and sauté for a few more minutes.

Add rutabaga, water and no chicken base. Bring to a boil.

Add the wine, parsley and coconut water.

Lower the heat to low and cook for about 15 more minutes, until the rutabaga is completely softened. Purée the soup using a hand blender.

Garnish with fresh parsley and serve.

Yield

4-6 *servings*

1 TSP	olive oil
1	onion, thinly chopped
1	carrot, thinly chopped
1	parsnip, thinly chopped
2	celery stalks, thinly chopped
2 TBSP	semolina flour
1 TBSP	shawarma spice
2 C	black-eyed peas, soaked overnight and drained
1 TBSP	vegetable base
5 C	boiling water
1	bunch fresh cilantro, chopped
+	salt
+	pepper

BLACK-EYED PEA SOUP

Although their name might suggest otherwise, black-eyed peas are actually beans. As such, they are loaded with protein, fiber, vitamin K, vitamin B, vitamin A, and potassium. All of these vitamins and nutrients are essential for a plant-based diet, so getting them through legumes on a daily basis is important.

This soup, paired with a glass of red wine and a crunchy baguette is sure to satisfy any cravings while simultaneously fulfilling daily nutrient requirements.

Check out my tip on how to soak and cook beans (page 218).

In a large soup pot on medium heat, add olive oil, onion, salt and pepper. Sauté for a few minutes.

Add carrot, parsnip and celery stalks. Continue to sauté for a few minutes.

Add semolina flour and shawarma spices. Sauté for a couple more minutes.

Add water, vegetable base, and black-eyed peas.

Bring to a boil then lower to a simmer for about 30-40 minutes, until the beans are completely softened.

Add cilantro and serve hot with a nice crunchy baguette.

Yield

6-8 *servings*

1 TBSP	olive oil
1	large onion, chopped
1	eggplant, cut into cubes
1	small yam, grated
1	parsnip, cut into cubes
2	small zucchinis, cut into cubes
1 TBSP	Old Bay Seasoning
1 TBSP	tomato paste
2 TBSP	ketchup
1/2 TSP	cumin powder
1 TBSP	no chicken base
1 TSP	paprika
7 C	water
+	salt
+	pepper

DECADENT EGGPLANT SOUP

This soup is loaded with vegetables and loaded with flavors--even a bit spicy. Eggplant, onion, yam, zucchini, and parsnip all come together in a lovely, creamy soup.

In a cast iron soup pot on medium heat, add olive oil, onion, salt and pepper. Sauté until translucent.

Add eggplant. Sauté for a few more minutes

Add yam, parsnip and zucchinis. Add more salt and pepper. Sauté for a few more minutes.

Add Old Bay Seasoning, tomato paste, ketchup, cumin, no chicken base, paprika, and lastly add water. Bring to a boil and then lower to a simmer. Cook until all vegetables are tender, about 30 minutes.

Blend with a hand blender until smooth.

Serve warm.

Yield

4-6 *servings*

10-12   celery stalks, thinly sliced
1/4 C   candied walnuts, chopped

dressing:

1 TBSP   vegan mayo
1 TBSP   vegan sweet chili sauce
   +   juice of 1/2 lemon
   +   salt
   +   pepper

CELERY SALAD

Celery was never my first choice when it came to vegetables, until my mom shared her new recipe for celery salad. I'm very open to trying new things, so I gave it a shot, and of course, put my own spin on it. I couldn't believe how flavorful and fresh a two-ingredient salad could be.

What's more fantastic is when you think about the health benefits of celery, you'll like it even more. Celery is known for its anti-inflammatory benefits, low calories and high level of antioxidants. It's better to eat it as fresh as possible in order to capture all its active nutrients.

Mix all dressing ingredients in a bowl using a whisk.

Pour the dressing over the celery and mix well.

Add walnuts on top and serve.

8   *servings*

 GF

1   head of cauliflower, grated in a food processor
1 C carrots, grated
1/2 C parsley, chopped
1/2 C mint, chopped
1/4 C walnuts, chopped
8   roma tomatoes with flesh scooped out (use a spoon to scoop)

dressing:

1 TBSP olive oil
  * juice and zest of one lemon
  * juice and zest of one orange
1 TBSP pure maple syrup
  * salt
  * pepper

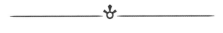

You can keep the tomato flesh and use it later in a sauce. Freeze in a ziplock bag to store for longer.

CAULIFLOWER SALAD STUFFED TOMATOES

Mix all the salad ingredients in a bowl.

Mix all the dressing ingredients in another bowl using a whisk.

Pour the dressing over the cauliflower salad and mix.

Trim the bottoms of the tomatoes so they stand upright.

Stuff the tomatoes and serve.

Yield

4-6 *servings*

 GF

1 C quinoa
1 1/2 C water
+ salt
1 english cucumber, thinly cubed
4 tomatoes, thinly cubed
3 carrots: red, orange and white, thinly cubed
1/4 C mint and parsley leaves, thinly chopped

dressing:

+ juice and zest of one lemon
2 TBSP olive oil
+ salt
+ pepper

Most Israelis eat an Israeli salad every single day—breakfast, lunch or dinner. I've noticed that in hot weather countries, people tend to eat lighter meals and combine more vegetables and fruits into their diets. I gave this a twist and included quinoa to the classic Israeli salad. I also added colorful carrots that I found at my local farmers market, which builds another layer of flavor and color. Be creative, add more fresh vegetables. You can't go wrong with this. It really is better than taking vitamins.

ISRAELI SALAD WITH QUINOA

Cook quinoa, water and salt on low heat until the quinoa has absorbed all the water.

Let cool completely.

Place all chopped vegetables into a large salad bowl. Add cooled quinoa, chopped mint and parsley.

Mix dressing ingredients and pour over the salad.

Mix and serve.

4-6 *servings*

2 C   fresh Brussels sprouts
1/4 C   cranberries
3   pieces dried mango,
        sliced into small strips
1/3 C   chopped, roasted, and
        salted mixed nuts

dressing:

1 TBSP   pure maple syrup
1 TSP   apple cider vinegar
1 TSP   horseradish mustard
1 TSP   olive oil
    +   zest and juice of one
        lemon
    +   salt
    +   pepper

FRESH BRUSSELS SPROUTS SALAD WITH DRIED MANGO & CRANBERRIES

Brussels sprouts are my husband's favorite vegetable. He grew up in England and his mother used to make them all the time.

In fall and early winter, Oregon farms harvest outstanding Brussels sprouts. I recently bought a whole head—which is huge!—and used it in a few different recipes.

Although it is time consuming to peel the outer layers of a Brussels sprout, it is so worth it in the end. The salad is very colorful and the texture is excellent.

Using a paring knife, cut around the core of each Brussels sprout, gently removing the outer leaves.

Only use the first two or three outer layers of leaves. Reserve the rest for another purpose. (I used mine in a chopped Brussels sprouts salad, which you'll see on the next page.) It is time consuming but well worth it.

In a salad bowl, add the Brussels sprouts leaves, cranberries, mango and nuts.

Mix all the dressing ingredients.

Pour the dressing over the salad. Mix and serve.

Yield

4-6 *servings*

6 C Brussels sprouts, thinly chopped
1 apple peeled and cubed
9 dried plums, thinly sliced

dressing:

+ zest and juice of one lemon
+ zest and juice of 2 clementines
1 TBSP pure maple syrup
1 TBSP vegan mayonnaise
1 TSP olive oil
+ salt
+ pepper

CHOPPED RAW BRUSSELS SPROUTS, APPLE & DRIED PLUM SALAD

The combination of the chopped Brussels sprouts with the sweetness of the apple and dried plums is amazing, and even better the next day when all the flavors have soaked in. The dressing brings the salad's flavors to life—especially the zest of the clementines.

Mix all salad ingredients in a bowl.

Mix all dressing ingredients in another bowl using a whisk.

Pour the dressing over the salad and serve.

4-6 *servings*

- **2 C** soaked bulgur (1 cup dry bulgur soaked in 1 cup boiling water)
- **1** carrot, thinly cubed
- **2** roma tomatoes, thinly cubed
- **1** yellow pepper, thinly cubed
- **1** red bell pepper, thinly cubed
- **2** green onions, thinly chopped
- **1/2 C** fresh parsley, chopped
- **1 TBSP** hemp seeds.

dressing:

- **+** juice and zest of one lemon
- **1 TBSP** olive oil
- **+** salt
- **+** pepper

Tabbouleh salad is a classic Middle Eastern dish. It is a very refreshing salad, lemony, super healthy and delicious. It is a great side dish or appetizer that is colorful and aromatic.

In this recipe I kept the calories on the low side by using less bulgur and more veggies. You can always use more bulgur if you prefer.

For a gluten free option, replace the bulgur with cooked quinoa.

BULGUR TABBOULEH SALAD

Mix all salad ingredients together.

Mix all dressing ingredients and pour over the salad.

serving suggestion:

Serve a scoop of tabbouleh on whole leaves of fresh romaine lettuce.

SUMAC-SPICED SPINACH & VEGGIE SALAD

Yield

4-6 *servings*   (GF)

3-4 C	fresh baby spinach
1	yam, peeled, cubed and roasted with olive oil, salt & pepper
1	red bell pepper, cubed
1	persian cucumber, cubed
1/2 C	fresh cooked corn
1/4 C	pinto beans, soaked overnight, cooked and drained (measurement refers to the cooked beans)
1/4 C	garbanzo beans, soaked overnight, cooked and drained (measurement refers to the cooked beans)
10	black kalamata olives, pitted and sliced
+	handful of fresh parsley, chopped

dressing:

1 TBSP	olive oil
+	juice of 1 lemon
+	salt
+	pepper

sprinkle on top:

1 TSP	sumac

Layer salad on a wide serving platter.

Start with spinach. Follow with yams, red bell pepper, cucumber, corn, pinto beans, garbanzo beans, olives and parsley.

In another mixing bowl, add all dressing ingredients. Whisk to combine.

Pour dressing over salad and sprinkle with sumac. Serve.

Salad for lunch is always a great option. It is light and naturally gives you the energy you need to keep going.

Growing up in Israel, I was exposed to a common spice called sumac, which is a reddish-purple berry that is dried and ground. Sumac (meaning "blush" in Arabic) has a wonderful lemony flavor that compliments many dishes, such as tofu, hummus, tahini, vegetables and more. Sumac is also known for its antioxidants, low glycemic index and low cholesterol.

Not only is sumac good for you, it also adds spice to a salad. You can order sumac online or find it in any Mediterranean grocery store.

Check out my tip on how to soak and cook beans (page 218).

Yield

4-6 *servings*

 (GF)

4 C	mixed greens: kale, spinach, arugula
1/2	english cucumber, cubed
3	beets, cooked and cubed
1 C	alfalfa and clover sprouts
3	pomelo segments
1/4 C	roasted pine nuts

dressing:

1/2 C	fresh cilantro, chopped
1 TBSP	olive oil
+	zest and juice of 1/2 lemon
1 TBSP	vegan mayonnaise
+	salt
+	pepper

When pomelos are in season, I buy them all the time. They remind me of my childhood. My parents have a pomelo tree in their backyard, and my mom used to peel them for me when I was a kid.

Pomelos in Israel are very different than the ones you find in the U.S.. In Israel they are white inside and very sweet. Here, the inside fruit is red and more sour.

Most of the time our family just eats them plain, but sometimes, I'll combine them to make a dish like this salad.

WINTER GREENS SALAD WITH BEETS, POMELO & PINE NUTS

In a salad bowl, first lay the greens, then cucumber, beets, sprouts, pomelo and pine nuts.

Mix all the dressing ingredients separately and pour over the salad. Mix and serve.

Yield

4-6 *servings*

 GF

7	roma tomatoes, cut into cubes
8	leaves of fresh basil, chopped
1/4 C	roasted pine nuts

dressing:

+	juice of 1/2 lemon
1 TSP	balsamic vinaigrette
2 TSP	olive oil
+	salt
+	pepper

TOMATO BASIL SALAD

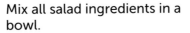

Tomato salad is a classic, especially on summer days. It is so refreshing, so light, and so juicy.

I love fresh tomatoes in a salad—combined with fresh basil and pine nuts—even better. Just a few ingredients develop this salad's bold flavor. In this case, less is more.

Mix all salad ingredients in a bowl.

Mix all dressing ingredients in another bowl using a whisk.

Pour dressing over the salad, mix and serve.

Yield

4-6 *servings*

 GF

1 bunch flat leaf parsley, chopped
1 bunch curly parsley, chopped
1 green pear, thinly cubed
1/4 C roasted sunflower seeds
1/4 C honey roasted walnuts, chopped

dressing:

+ juice of 1/2 lemon
2 TSP pure maple syrup
3 TSP olive oil
+ salt
+ pepper

PARSLEY PEAR SALAD

Parsley is one of the healthiest greens around. It is loaded with vitamins such as Vitamin K, C and B12. It is very good at boosting your immune system. Not only is it good for you, but it is also delicious.

In a bowl add all salad ingredients.

In another bowl, mix all dressing ingredients.

Pour the dressing over the salad, mix and serve.

Yield

6-8 *servings*

1 medium cauliflower, separated into florets
1 yellow pepper, cut into strips
1 red pepper, cut into strips
1 fennel bulb, sliced into circles
1 C mini carrots
2 TSP salt
+ juice of 2 lemons

Pickled veggies are a must in every Mediterranean kitchen. They are crunchy, flavorful, and a great addition to any meal. Serve as an appetizer or even a snack.

My boys in particular love pickles, and this quick recipe delivers pickles in hours that are as good as those that take 2 weeks. Although it is recommended to let the vegetables pickle for 24 hours, they will be ready even before, as long as you mix them well. Turning the bag or container upside down a few times will help cover all the veggies evenly with the lemon-salt mixture.

You can also use these pickles in a kale salad. Cut your kale very thin and add a cup of chopped pickles. Mix them together, add some pepper and some olive oil, and you've got the most amazing salad.

QUICK PICKLED VEGGIES

Place prepared veggies, lemon juice and salt in an airtight container or ziplock bag.

Shake the container, turning it upside down a few times as well. Store in the fridge overnight.

In the morning, shake again and turn the container upside down to cover the veggies evenly with the lemon-salt mixture.

In 24 hours or less, it's ready. Great addition to any meal and great as a snack.

Yield

6-8 *servings*

 GF

1 C	quinoa
1 1/2 C	water
1/2 TSP	salt
1	large fresh beet, peeled and grated
1/2 C	raw walnuts, chopped
1/4 C	cranberries

dressing:

1 TBSP	olive oil
+	juice of 1 lemon
1 TSP	pure maple syrup
+	salt
+	pepper

QUINOA BEET SALAD

I love quinoa cooked and served in many ways—warm as a risotto-like side dish, in soup, or as a cold salad—the variations are endless. Beets are abundant in fiber, vitamin C, vitamin B, potassium, and manganese, which all help protect the heart, regulate digestive health, and reduce inflammation in the body. The beets, together with the flavor and texture of the quinoa, provide a well-balanced meal.

Start by cooking the quinoa in salt water on low heat. When the quinoa has absorbed all the water, it's ready. Let cool completely.

Add grated beets, walnuts and cranberries to the cooled quinoa.

Mix all the dressing ingredients in a mixing bowl using a whisk.

Pour the dressing over the quinoa.

Mix and serve.

Yield

9 *rolls*

1 package organic soba japanese green tea noodles (7 oz/200 g)
1 package of organic sprouted extra firm tofu (7.5 oz/218 g), cut into strips
3 long carrots, cut into thin strips
1 package clover sprouts (4 oz/113 g)
2 C green or red cabbage, thinly shredded
9 Vietnamese rice papers, 31 cm diameter or smaller

peanut sauce:

1/2 C organic peanut butter
1/8 C vegan sweet chili sauce
1 C coconut water

This is a lovely starter to any meal. I call it a "condensed salad," because it's easy to eat, and you don't feel guilty afterwards. It's tasty, especially with my low-calorie version of the peanut sauce made with coconut water instead of coconut milk and organic peanut butter that contains only peanuts and salt. This creates a much lighter and healthier sauce. Use the sauce as a dip or a great add-on protein for salads.

SALAD ROLLS WITH WARM PEANUT SAUCE

Cook the soba noodles according to the instructions on the package. Set aside.

Fill a large bowl with lukewarm water and line up the rest of the ingredients at your work station.

Start assembling.

Dip the rice paper one at a time in the warm water, then place on a large cutting board. Start by adding a small handful of noodles. Top with 2-3 pieces of tofu, a few strips of carrots, and a small handful of cabbage and sprouts. Fold the edge of the rice paper closest to you to the center, then fold in both sides and roll tight. Cut diagonally just before serving.

peanut sauce:

In a saucepan on medium heat, add all ingredients, mix with a whisk until thickened and well blended.

Yield

6-8 *servings*

GF

1   head of green cabbage, chopped
1   package of mung bean sprouts (12 oz/340 g)
5   radishes, thinly sliced
2 TBSP   toasted sesame seeds
+   zest of one orange

dressing:

1/4 C   gf low sodium soy sauce/tamari
1/4 C   vegan sweet chili sauce
1/4 C   rice vinegar
1 TBSP   sesame oil
1 TBSP   pure maple syrup
1 TBSP   brown sugar
1 TSP   fresh ginger, grated
+   salt
+   pepper

serving:

+   black sesame seeds

Cabbage and sprouts add so much crunch, flavor, and freshness to any dish. They are loaded with nutrients, so they can be eaten without guilt. The Asian dressing completes this salad, and the sesame seeds add the finishing touch.

ASIAN CABBAGE SLAW

Add all salad ingredients to a large mixing bowl.

Add all dressing ingredients to a small mixing bowl. Mix well using a whisk and pour over the salad.

Toss and serve on a large plate, then sprinkle with black sesame seeds.

Yield

4-6 *servings*

 GF

---

3 C	baby kale, pre-washed
1 C	red cabbage, chopped
1	red bell pepper, cubed
1/2	avocado, cubed
1	mango, peeled and cubed
1 TBSP	hemp seeds
1/4 C	dry roasted slivered almonds

dressing:

1 TSP	olive oil
+	juice of 1 lemon
1 TSP	pure maple syrup
+	salt
+	pepper

The possible variations for a salad are endless. I always strive to make my salads more unique and interesting to the palette. In this recipe, I include protein (almonds), good fat (avocado), antioxidants (kale, cabbage) as well as a superfood (hemp seeds) and a little sweetness (mango), to complete the balance.

BABY KALE SALAD WITH HEMP SEEDS & DRY ROASTED ALMONDS

Mix all salad ingredients in a bowl.

Mix all dressing ingredients in a separate bowl using a whisk.

Pour the dressing over the salad, mix and serve.

BURGERS
& Patties

Yield

12 *patties*

1 TSP   olive oil
    2   green onions, chopped
    5   celery stalks, chopped
    1   clove of garlic, minced
1 TSP   cumin powder
1 TSP   turmeric
  1 C   cooked carrots
    1   small cooked yam
    1   small piece of cooked
        rutabaga, about 1/2 cup
        (substitute cooked
        potato for rutabaga if
        necessary)
    1   package organic
        sprouted extra-firm tofu
        (15.5 oz/439 g)
2 TSP   nutritional yeast
2 TBSP flaxseed meal
1 TBSP gf soy sauce/tamari
1/2 C   gf panko bread crumbs
1 TSP   pure maple syrup
1 TSP   Old Bay Seasoning
  1 C   gf old fashioned oats
    ✦   salt
    ✦   pepper
    ✦   olive oil spray

It took a lot of time and effort to perfect a recipe for a good tofu burger. The flavor, most likely the cumin, reminds me of falafel.

My mom always said, "If people say it's good, but plates stay full, don't believe them. Only if the plates are empty and clean, you know your food was good." By the end of this meal, my kids' plates were completely clean.

TOFU & VEGGIE PATTIES

Heat oven to 375° F.

In a nonstick pan on medium heat, add olive oil, onions, celery, garlic, salt, pepper, cumin and turmeric. Sauté until tender.

In a food processor, add the sautéed onion-celery mixture along with cooked carrots, cooked yam, cooked rutabaga, tofu, nutritional yeast, flaxseed, soy sauce, bread crumbs, pure maple syrup, Old Bay Seasoning and oats.

Pulse until smooth and sticky.

Line a baking sheet with parchment paper.

Using an ice cream scoop, place evenly spaced portions of the mixture on the baking sheet and flatten them with wet hands. Dip the scoop in water in between portions to prevent sticking.

Spray the top of the patties with olive oil and bake for about 20-30 minutes, until golden brown.

Let sit for 5-10 minutes before serving.

CAULIFLOWER ZUCCHINI PATTIES

Yield

17 *patties*

- 1 head of cauliflower, steamed
- 1 medium zucchini, cubed
- 1/2 C raw cashews, soaked for 1/2 hour, and drained
- 2 flax eggs (mix 2 tablespoons flaxseed meal and 6 tablespoons lukewarm water. Let stand for 10-15 minutes.)
- 1/2 C cornmeal
- 1/2 C gf panko bread crumbs
- 1 C fresh cilantro, chopped
- 1 TBSP olive oil
- 1 TBSP nutritional yeast
- + salt
- + pepper
- + olive oil spray

If you don't feel like spending a whole day in the kitchen, a vegan burger is a really easy dinner option that's made with fresh ingredients, tons of flavor, and vibrant colors.

Heat oven to 375° F.

In a food processor add all the ingredients, pulse until smooth.

Line a baking sheet with parchment paper. Using an ice cream scoop, place evenly spaced portions of the mixture on the baking sheet and flatten them with wet hands. Dip the scoop in water in between portions to prevent sticking.

Spray the top of the patties with olive oil and bake for about 30-40 minutes, until golden brown.

Let sit for 5-10 minutes before serving.

Yield

18 *patties*

GF

1 TBSP	olive oil
1	onion, chopped or 2 leeks, chopped
4 C	cooked green lentils
1 C	cooked tricolor quinoa
3	carrots, grated
1 TSP	turmeric
1 TSP	cumin
2 TBSP	hemp seeds
1 TBSP	flaxseed
2 TBSP	flaxseed meal
+	salt
+	pepper
+	olive oil spray

Lentil burgers with tricolor quinoa is truly the closest thing to the flavor of a hamburger. They are loaded with superfood ingredients, such as hemp seeds and flax seeds, as well as proteins and vitamins.

Try pre-making and freezing them instead of buying ready-made vegan burgers. You will control the amount of sodium and the freshness of the ingredients. By adding fresh vegetables and tahini sauce (page 46), you'll have a complete, nutritious meal.

Leeks always carry dirt, therefore, they need to be soaked. You want to slice into rings first, then separate and place into a large bowl of water. Next, dry in a salad spinner or with a clean towel.

QUINOA & LENTIL PATTIES

Heat oven to 375° F.

In a nonstick pan on medium heat, sauté onion with olive oil, salt and pepper until golden and translucent. Set aside.

In a bowl, add cooked lentils, cooked quinoa, carrots, turmeric, cumin, hemp seeds, flaxseeds, flaxseed meal and the sautéed onions. Mix well.

Use a hand blender to blend about half of the mixture in the same bowl. You want to keep some of the mixture unblended to maintain the texture of the patties. Mix this final mixture together using a spatula or by hand.

Line a baking sheet with parchment paper. Using an ice cream scoop, place evenly spaced portions of the mixture on the baking sheet and flatten them with wet hands. Dip the scoop in water in between portions to prevent sticking.

Spray the patties with olive oil and bake for 20-25 minutes until golden brown.

Let sit for about 5-10 minutes before serving.

Eat with your favorite bun and veggies.

Yield

13 *burgers*

1 TSP olive oil
1 onion, chopped
3 cloves garlic, minced
1 package white mushrooms (24 oz/679 g), washed and sliced
1 TSP dried thyme
1 TSP Old Bay Seasoning
1 TBSP dried parsley
2 C soaked bulgur (1 cup dried bulgur in 1 cup boiling water)
1 C panko bread crumbs
1 TBSP nutritional yeast
2 flax eggs (mix 2 tablespoons flaxseed meal with 6 tablespoons water. Let soak for about 10 minutes.)
+ salt
+ pepper
+ olive oil spray

MUSHROOM BULGUR BURGERS

The bulgur in these mushroom burgers makes the texture really fluffy and light. I like mushroom chunks in my burger, and for this reason I use a knife to chop the mushrooms instead of a food processor.

I serve this burger on a slice of roasted butternut squash. The sweetness of the butternut squash and the saltiness of the mushroom burger create a perfect combination of flavor.

Top it with avocado and tahini sauce (page 46) and enjoy.

Heat oven to 375° F.

Line a baking sheet with parchment paper.

In a nonstick pan on medium heat, add olive oil, onion, garlic, salt and pepper. Sauté for a couple of minutes until translucent.

Add mushrooms, dried thyme, Old Bay Seasoning and dried parsley. Sauté until most of the liquid has evaporated. Set aside.

In a separate bowl, add the soaked bulgur, bread crumbs, nutritional yeast, flax eggs and the mushroom mixture. Mix all together.

Use an ice cream scoop to portion evenly sized burgers. Shape the burgers by pressing gently with a spatula. Spray the top of the burgers with olive oil and bake for about 20 minutes, until golden brown.

Let sit for 5-10 minutes before serving.

Yield

15 *burgers*

 GF

1 C	fresh parsley
1/2 C	carrots
1 TBSP	olive oil
1	large onion, chopped
1	clove garlic, minced
+	organic crimini mushrooms (6 oz/170 g), chopped
4-5	stems of fresh thyme
4 C	brown and black rice together, cooked, divided
1 1/2 C	black beans, cooked, divided
1 TBSP	cumin
1 TBSP	sweet paprika
1 TSP	turmeric
+	salt
+	pepper
+	olive oil spray

The key to making this burger successful is the large sautéed onion and mushrooms. These make it fluffy and delicious. Serve on whole grain hamburger buns, and spread with smoky vegan mayo (see page 103).

Check out my tip on how to soak and cook beans (page 218).

BROWN RICE & BLACK BEAN BURGERS

Heat oven to 375° F.

Line a baking sheet with parchment paper. Set aside.

In a food processor, add parsley and carrots. Pulse until thinly chopped. Pour into a mixing bowl. Set aside.

In a nonstick pan on medium heat, add olive oil, onion, garlic, salt and pepper. Sauté until translucent.

Add the fresh thyme and mushrooms. Sauté until golden and tender. Add to carrot-parsley mixture.

In a food processor, pulse 2 cups (of the 4 cups) of the brown-black rice and 1 cup (of the 1 1/2 cups) of the black beans until you reach a paste consistency. Pour into the carrot-parsley-mushroom mixture.

Add the remaining brown rice, black beans, cumin, paprika, turmeric, salt and pepper. Mix well with your hands until evenly distributed.

With wet hands, form evenly sized patties and place on baking sheet.

Spray the patties with olive oil and bake for about 20-25 minutes.

Serve with your favorite bun.

Yield

12 *hot dogs*

1 C	yellow split pea
2 C	boiling water
+	salt
3 1/2 C	cooked quinoa
1/2 TSP	ground cumin
1/2 TSP	turmeric
1/4 TSP	coriander
1/4 TSP	cardamom
1/2 TSP	garlic powder
2 TSP	paprika
1 TBSP	arrowroot
2 TBSP	gf soy sauce/tamari
1 TSP	vegetable base
2 TBSP	olive oil
1/4 TSP	liquid smoke
+	olive oil spray
+	salt
+	pepper

Vegan hot dogs are a great replacement for the real thing. These have a smoky flavor, a smooth texture, and are guilt-free. Add ketchup, mustard and pickles on your favorite bun. They are super healthy, loaded with fiber, vitamins and good, low-in-fat protein.

Plus, they're pretty easy to make, and they freeze well—a great homemade, nutritious lunch or easy dinner option during that busy work week. Just thaw and warm up and they are ready to eat.

HOT DOGS

Heat oven to 375° F.

In a saucepan, add yellow split peas, water and salt. Cook until all the water has evaporated.

In a food processor, add quinoa, cooked split pea, cumin, turmeric, coriander, cardamom, garlic powder, paprika, arrowroot, soy sauce, vegetable base, olive oil, salt, pepper and liquid smoke. Blend until very smooth. Set aside.

Prepare (12) 12" x 5" sheets of aluminum foil. Lay on a surface and spray with olive oil.

The mixture should be enough for about 12 hot dogs. You can use a large ice cream scoop to help measure evenly-sized portions.

Place one scoop of mixture on each sheet of aluminum foil. With wet hands, spread out the mixture to approximately the length of a hot dog. Roll in the aluminum foil and twist the sides like a candy wrapper.

Bake for about 25 minutes. Let cool and form before serving.

You can also freeze and eat them later. Serve on your favorite bun with quality mustard, ketchup and spicy pickles.

100

SUPERFOOD VEGGIE PATTIES

Yield

12-14 *patties* GF

1	sweet potato
4	green onions
2	zucchinis
4	carrots
2	tomatoes
1	bunch of fresh parsley, chopped
1/4 C	garbanzo bean flour
2 TBSP	flaxseed meal
2 TBSP	hemp seeds
2 TBSP	chia seeds
+	salt
+	pepper
1 TBSP	olive oil
+	olive oil spray

Heat oven to 375° F.

Line a baking sheet with parchment paper.

In a food processor with a grater attachment, grate sweet potato, onion, zucchini, carrots and tomato.

Pour into a bowl and add the rest of the ingredients. Mix well.

Form evenly sized patties and place on baking sheet.

Spray with olive oil and bake for about 30 minutes, until golden brown.

Serve warm over sautéed greens.

Superfood veggie patties are the ultimate guilt-free dinner.

Garbanzo bean flour is rich in protein and will keep you satisfied longer. Along with hemp seeds, chia seeds, flaxseed meal (which are all considered superfoods) and fresh vegetables, you get a well-rounded, nutrient-packed meal.

Yield

1 C   *mayo*

1 C   vegan mayonnaise
1 TBSP   smoked paprika
1 TBSP   olive oil
   +   salt

SMOKY MAYO

This recipe is super easy, full of flavor and an upgrade for any sandwich.

It is great for marinating tofu or pairing it with your favorite vegan burger.

You can also use this smoky mayo to add a little kick to your salad dressings.

Mix all the ingredients and keep in a mason jar in the fridge.

Yield

14-16 *patties*

 GF

sauce:

1	clove of garlic
1	can tomato sauce (15 oz/425 g)
1	can fire roasted red peppers 12 oz
1/4 C	fresh cilantro
1/4 C	fresh basil
1 TBSP	pure maple syrup
1 TSP	hot paprika paste or hot sauce
2 C	water
+	salt
+	pepper

patties:

1 C	dried peas, soaked in 1 1/2 cups water for 3 hours or more
1/2 C	water
1 TBSP	olive oil
1 C	fresh parsley
3/4 C	roasted mixed nuts
1 1/2 TBSP	flaxseed meal
1	clove of garlic, minced
1/2 C	gf panko bread crumbs
+	salt
+	pepper

Dried peas are packed with fiber, can lower your cholesterol, and manage blood sugar disorders. They are also great for the digestive system and the heart, not to mention a good source of protein, manganese, folate, vitamin B1, potassium and phosphorus.

DRIED PEA PATTIES IN PICANTE RED SAUCE

sauce:

In a food processor, add all sauce ingredients and blend until completely smooth. Pour the sauce into a large cast iron skillet and turn to low heat.

patties:

Strain dried peas and wash under running water, and then add to a food processor with water, olive oil, parsley, nuts, flaxseed, garlic, panko, salt and pepper. Blend until smooth.

Set aside.

Dip an ice cream scoop into a cup of water and then portion mixture into evenly sized patties.

Gently place patties into the sauce. Cover and cook for at least 1/2 hour or more. Shake the pan from time to time to ensure that the patties don't stick to the bottom of the pan.

Serve warm with soft polenta (page 139).

Yield

6-8 *servings*

- 1 package sprouted organic firm tofu (14 oz/397 g)
- 1 package frozen organic corn (16 oz/453 g), thawed
- 3 TBSP low sodium soy sauce/tamari
- 1 1/2 TBSP tahini paste
- 1/2 C organic sprouted spelt flour
- 1 C panko bread crumbs
- 1 C sautéed onion
- + pepper
- + salt
- 1 TSP pure maple syrup

topping:

- + olive oil spray
- + panko bread crumbs

Corn schnitzel was by far my favorite childhood lunch choice for years. I love corn so much—the sweetness, the texture, the creaminess of it. I recreated my own homemade version, and it turned out delicious. Crunchy, sweet, salty and decadent. I like to dip mine in homemade thousand island dressing—just mix ketchup with vegan mayo. It's a great kid-friendly meal. Pair with a zesty tabbouleh salad (page 82), and you'll have a balanced, healthy dinner on the table.

These can be easily transformed into gf by substituting spelt flour with gf flour blend and using gf panko bread crumbs.

BAKED CORN SCHNITZEL

Heat oven to 375° F.

Line a large baking sheet with parchment paper. Set aside.

In a food processor, add tofu (break into pieces before adding), 2 cups corn (set the rest aside), soy sauce, tahini, spelt flour, panko bread crumbs, sautéed onion, pure maple syrup, salt and pepper. Blend until you reach a smooth, sticky batter.

In a bowl, combine the reserved corn with the batter.

Prepare two bowls: one with bread crumbs and one with water.

Use an ice cream scoop to create evenly sized patties (dip the ice cream scoop in water to prevent sticking). Dip the patties in bread crumbs. Repeat with the rest of the batter.

Lay the patties on the baking sheet and spray with olive oil. Bake for about 30 minutes or until golden brown.

11-12 *cakes*

1 C sweet brown rice cooked with 2 cups of water
3 green onions, chopped
3 TBSP nutritional yeast
2 TBSP roasted sesame seeds
+ salt
+ pepper

topping:

1 C gf panko bread crumbs
+ olive oil spray

A great way to get your daily dose of whole grains is by eating brown rice. Sweet brown rice is basically a sticky brown rice. So that means no empty calories, just whole grains that taste similar to sushi white rice.

I was happy when I first found sweet brown rice at the market, and was very excited to create a risotto-style rice cake with it. My kids loved them and didn't leave a single piece for dad. They were all over them, and I understand why. The flavor is mild, the texture soft and chewy, and the bread crumbs create a perfect crunch. I serve them as a side dish with my Spicy Soy Curl Chraime (page 132).

CHEESY BROWN RICE CAKES, RISOTTO STYLE

Heat oven to 375° F.

Line a baking sheet with parchment paper.

In a mixing bowl, add cooked brown rice, green onions, nutritional yeast, sesame seeds, salt and pepper. Mix well.

Scoop evenly sized portions of the mixture with an ice cream scoop. Place the bread crumbs in a mixing bowl. Dip the rice cakes in the bread crumbs bowl to cover and place on baking sheet. Spray with olive oil and bake for about 20 minutes until golden brown.

MAIN
Dishes

STUFFED MINI PEPPERS IN COCONUT-LEEK CREAMY SAUCE

Yield

4-6 *servings*   GF

---

12   mini colorful peppers, trimmed and seeded

sauce:

1 TSP   olive oil
3 C   leeks, chopped
1 TSP   fresh ginger, grated
1   clove garlic, minced
1   can light coconut milk, (14 oz/400 ml)
1 TBSP   gf mellow white miso paste
+   salt
+   pepper

filling:

1 TSP   olive oil
1   jalapeño, seeded, chopped
1   celery stalk, chopped
1   carrot, grated
1/2 TSP   Old Bay Seasoning
1 C   cooked tricolor quinoa
+   salt
+   pepper

Heat oven to 375° F.

sauce:

In a nonstick pan, add olive oil, leeks, ginger and garlic. Sauté on medium heat until tender and fragrant.

Add coconut milk and miso paste. Reduce heat to low and cover. Let cook for about 20 minutes. Blend until smooth with a hand blender. Transfer to a square Pyrex dish.

filling:

In a nonstick pan on medium heat, add olive oil, jalapeño, celery, carrot, salt and pepper. Sauté for a couple of minutes.

Add Old Bay Seasoning and cooked quinoa. Sauté for a few more minutes, until the flavors combine. Set aside.

Use a spoon to stuff the filling into the peppers. You can pack them pretty tight. Lay the peppers directly on the sauce

and cover with aluminum foil. Bake for about 30 minutes. Remove the aluminum foil and bake for an additional 10-15 minutes. Let set for a few minutes before serving.

---------- ----------

You can use this same filling to stuff a variety of other vegetables. I stuffed portobello mushrooms, and baked it in the oven for 20-30 minutes at 350°F until the top was golden brown.

Leeks always carry dirt, therefore, they need to be soaked. You want to slice into rings first, then separate and place into a large bowl of water. Next, dry in a salad spinner or with a clean towel.

---------- ----------

Yield

14-16 *balls*

black & brown rice balls:

1 C	brown sweet rice
1 C	black rice/forbidden rice
4 C	water
+	salt

zucchini & garbanzo beans:

1 TSP	olive oil
6	zucchinis, cubed
1/2 C	garbanzo beans, cooked
+	salt
+	pepper

rice ball topping:

| 1 C | sesame seeds |

garnish:

| 1/4 C | parsley, chopped |

Brown sweet rice is basically a brown sticky rice—an excellent source of fiber with amazing texture, similar to risotto just without the oil and cheese.

Black rice, which I love, is nutty and sticky—it stays moist inside and keeps its shape. You can find it at your local Asian supermarket.

Check out my tip on how to soak and cook beans (page 218).

BLACK & BROWN RICE BALLS OVER ZUCCHINI & GARBANZO BEANS

Heat oven to 375° F.

Cook brown and black rice in water with a bit of salt. Set aside. Let cool.

In a nonstick pan on medium heat, add olive oil, zucchini, salt and pepper. Sauté until tender. Add garbanzo beans. Mix and set aside.

assemble the rice balls:

With a very small ice cream scoop, scoop even portions of the rice mix. Roll and firmly press into small rice balls with wet hands.

Divide and roll half of the balls in sesame seeds until covered.

Place both sets of balls on a baking sheet lined with parchment paper. Drizzle or brush the balls with olive oil and bake in the oven for about 15-20 minutes.

Place the zucchini-garbanzo bean mixture on a plate and place the rice balls on top. Garnish with parsley and serve.

Yield

8-10 *servings*

 GF

+ olive oil spray
2 medium eggplants, cut length-wise and oven-roasted with olive oil, salt and pepper (page 147)
2 C green lentils, washed and steamed
2-3 TBSP olive oil, divided
6 C butternut squash, cut into small cubes
1 TSP dried rosemary
1 medium onion, chopped
2 cloves garlic, chopped
+ salt
+ pepper

sauce:

2 C boiling water
1 can tomato paste (6 oz)
1 TBSP no chicken base

Tip: Steam the lentils and roast both the eggplant and butternut squash the day before. Keep in the fridge in airtight containers. This will make assembling the dish much quicker and easier. Planning is the key to creating a sophisticated dish in no time.

EGGPLANT, LENTIL & BUTTERNUT SQUASH MOUSSAKA

Spray olive oil on a large 10" x 14" Pyrex dish. Set aside.

On a baking sheet lined with parchment paper, lay the butternut squash. Drizzle with 2 tablespoons olive oil and top with rosemary, salt and pepper. Roast until golden but not completely soft.

In a nonstick pan on medium heat, add 1 tablespoon olive oil, onion, garlic, salt and pepper. Sauté until golden brown.

Add sauce ingredients to a sauce pan. Bring to a boil, then lower to a simmer and continue to cook for about 10 minutes. Set aside.

assembly:

First, lay the roasted eggplants on the bottom of the Pyrex dish. In order, top with steamed lentils, then onion mixture and then sauce. Lastly, spread the butternut squash evenly across the top and bake in the oven at 350° F for about 50-60 minutes.

Let set for 15 minutes before serving.

STUFFED PEPPERS

Yield

6 *stuffed peppers*

6 colorful bell peppers

filling:

1 TSP olive oil
4 C celery stalks, chopped
4 green onions, chopped
1/2 TSP turmeric
1/2 TSP sweet paprika
1/2 TSP onion powder
1/2 C pearl barley or brown rice
1/4 C quinoa
1 1/2 C boiling water
1 TBSP fresh cilantro or parsley, chopped
+ salt
+ pepper

sauce:

1 1/2 C boiling water
1 TBSP tomato paste
1 TSP no chicken base
1 TSP sweet paprika
1 TSP agave
+ salt
+ pepper

peppers:

Cut off the top of the peppers and scoop out the seeds.
Keep the top part to cover the peppers after you stuff them.

filling:

In a saucepan on medium heat, add olive oil, celery, green onions, salt and pepper. Sauté for a couple of minutes.

Add spices: turmeric, paprika, and onion powder. Sauté for a couple more minutes.

Add pearl barley, quinoa and boiling water. Lower heat and let simmer until all the water has evaporated. Add cilantro or parsley. Mix and set aside.

sauce:

Add all ingredients to a saucepan and bring to a boil. Set aside.

assembly:

Place the peppers in a wide pan. Try to fit them tightly against one another.

Stuff the peppers with the filling. Pour the sauce over the peppers and let simmer for an hour, or until the peppers are soft. Every 15 minutes, take a spoon and pour some sauce on the peppers to keep them moist and flavorful.

This dish can easily be transformed into gluten free by substituting rice instead of pearl barley.

Yield

4-6 *servings*

3	eggplants
4 C	colorful peppers, roasted, peeled and chopped
2	cloves garlic, minced
1 TBSP	olive oil
1 1/2 C	pearl barley or brown rice
3 C	water
1 TSP	no chicken base
1 TSP	turmeric
1 TSP	onion powder
+	salt
+	pepper
+	olive oil spray

to serve:

+ tahini sauce (page 46)

Eggplant is very versatile because it can be cooked in so many different ways in a variety of dishes. In this one, the softness of the eggplant is complimented by the crunch of the pearl barley and the tang of the roasted peppers.

Tip: After roasting the peppers (when they are still hot), place them in a ziplock bag, and let them steam until they cool. The steam will make them easier to peel.

Tip: you can easily substitute the pearl barley with rice and make this a gluten free recipe.

EGGPLANT ROLLS

for the eggplant:

Cut the eggplants lengthwise, 4-5 slices each. Trim the ends, spray with olive oil and sprinkle with salt and pepper. Roast in the oven until golden brown on both sides. Set aside.

for the filling:

Roast peppers in an oven or on the BBQ. Peel, remove the core with the seeds and chop. Set aside.

In a pot on medium heat, add one tablespoon olive oil, garlic and peppers. Sauté for a few minutes.

Add pearl barley, turmeric, no chicken base, onion powder, salt and pepper. Sauté for a couple more minutes.

Add water, bring to a boil, then lower heat to a simmer. Mix occasionally until most of the water has evaporated. It should remain moist.

pyrex dish assembly:

Roll about 1/2 cup pearl barley-pepper mixture inside of each slice of eggplant. Place side by side in the dish, seam-side down. Pour the rest of the filling between and around the rolls.

Cover with aluminum foil and bake at 375° F for about 1/2 hour.

Let set for 10 minutes before serving. Drizzle with tahini sauce (page 46) and serve.

6 *stuffed peppers*

1 TBSP	olive oil
1	medium onion, chopped
2	cloves garlic, minced
9	celery stalks, chopped
6	colorful bell peppers (red, yellow, orange)
1 TSP	onion powder
1 TSP	turmeric
1	can of tomato sauce (15 oz/425 g), divided between filling and sauce
1 C	dried red lentils, soaked in 1 1/2 cups water for about 3 hours

for the sauce:

1/2 CAN	tomato sauce
1 1/2 C	water
1 TSP	agave
+	salt
+	pepper

Growing up, my mom used to make stuffed peppers all the time. Of course, she used meat and rice in her recipe. I recreated them vegan-style and they turned out so flavorful! No meat is necessary to create an amazing stuffed pepper dish.

RED LENTIL STUFFED PEPPERS

In a nonstick pan on medium heat, add olive oil, onion, salt and pepper. Sauté until translucent.

Add garlic and celery. Sauté until tender.

Add onion powder and turmeric. Sauté for a couple of minutes.

Add tomato sauce (1/2 can) and the lentils with their liquids. Cook for about 5 minutes. Set aside.

peppers:

Cut off the top of the pepper below the stem and scoop out the seeds. Keep the tops and set aside.

Stuff the peppers with the mixture and then cover with the tops you removed earlier. Set aside.

Fit the peppers tightly together in a large pot.

Mix the sauce ingredients with a whisk and pour over the peppers.

Simmer for about 50-60 minutes until tender. While cooking, periodically spoon sauce from the bottom of the pot over the peppers to keep them moist and flavorful.

Serve warm with your favorite bread.

Yield

4-6 *servings*

2 TBSP   olive oil, divided
1   butternut squash, halved with seeds removed
1·TBSP   coconut oil
1   package organic sprouted extra firm tofu (15.5 oz/439 g), cut into cubes
1   medium onion, chopped
2   cloves garlic, minced
+   fresh mushrooms (about 12 oz) sliced
2   fresh sage leaves
2   stems fresh thyme
1 TBSP   gf soy sauce /tamari
1 TBSP   pure maple syrup
1 TSP   balsamic vinaigrette
+   salt
+   pepper

Butternut squash is one of my favorite vegetables. It is naturally sweet and light in calories. The texture of the crunchy tofu complements the softer texture of the mushrooms and the butternut squash, which is what makes this dish so perfect.

BUTTERNUT SQUASH STUFFED WITH MUSHROOMS & CRUNCHY TOFU

Heat oven to 350° F.

Brush or spray the inside of the halved butternut squash with 1 Tbsp olive oil. Sprinkle with salt and pepper. Make diagonal cuts in the squash's flesh with a knife and place face down on a baking sheet. Cook for about 30 minutes and then flip the pieces right-side up and roast until golden. Set aside.

In a nonstick pan on medium heat, add coconut oil and tofu. Sauté the tofu on each side until golden brown and crunchy. Sprinkle with salt. Remove from heat and set aside.

In the same pan, add 1 Tbsp olive oil, chopped onion, salt and pepper. Sauté until translucent.

Add garlic, mushrooms, sage, thyme, soy sauce, pure maple syrup and balsamic vinaigrette. Sauté until the liquid from the mushrooms has evaporated. Remove from heat and add tofu cubes. Mix gently.

Stuff the butternut squash and bake for about 10 minutes on 350° F until heated through.

Serve immediately.

4-6 *servings*

1 package organic sprouted extra firm tofu (15.5 oz/439 g), cut into triangles
+ olive oil spray

marinade:

5 TBSP coconut water
1 TBSP vegan sweet chili sauce
1 TBSP tamari
2 TBSP seasoned rice vinegar
1/2 TSP Sriracha hot sauce
2 TBSP ketchup
2 cloves garlic, minced
1 TSP gf organic mellow red miso
1/2 TSP turmeric
1 TSP fresh ginger, grated

crust:

1 C sesame seeds

peas and spinach:

1 package frozen organic spinach (10oz/284 g), thawed and drained
3 C frozen organic peas, thawed
1 C coconut water
+ salt
+ pepper

Tofu is one of the main sources of protein in a vegan diet. The options to work with tofu are endless. I tend to marinate the tofu because I like the flavors to soak in. This dish is a balanced meal, packed with nutritious protein, fiber and vitamins.

SESAME CRUSTED TOFU OVER PEAS & SPINACH

Heat oven to 375° F.

Line a baking sheet with parchment paper.

Pat the tofu dry and cut into triangles.

In a mixing bowl, add all marinade ingredients.

Add tofu to the marinade and let sit for 2 hours or overnight.

Coat the tofu in the sesame seeds and place on the baking sheet. Spray with olive oil and bake for about 30 minutes. Flip and broil for 5-7 minutes until golden brown. Set aside.

peas and spinach:

In a saucepan on medium heat, add spinach, peas, coconut water, salt and pepper. Bring to a boil, then lower the heat to a simmer and cook for about 10 minutes. Strain the liquids and set aside.

to serve:

Place tofu on a bed of peas and spinach. Serve warm.

Yield

6-8 *servings*

1 TBSP	olive oil
1	cabbage, thinly chopped
1 TBSP	garam masala
1 TBSP	curry powder
1 TSP	turmeric
2	carrots, sliced
2 C	white mushrooms (8 oz), sliced
2 C	water
2 C	coconut water
1 TBSP	no chicken base
1/4 C	cilantro, chopped, optional
1 1/2 C	cooked chickpeas
+	salt
+	pepper

CABBAGE STEW

In this recipe, it is important to let the cabbage simmer for a while until it's nice and soft. Let all the flavors combine and integrate—the more time the better. I like to use coconut water instead of coconut milk because coconut water is much lighter in calories and fat than coconut milk.

Check out my tip on how to soak and cook beans (page 218).

In a cast iron skillet on medium heat, add 1 tablespoon olive oil, cabbage, salt and pepper. Sauté for about 10 minutes.

Add garam masala, curry powder, and turmeric. Let simmer for about 10 minutes until all the flavors combine nicely.

Add carrots and mushrooms. Cook on high for a few minutes.

Add water, coconut water and no chicken base. Bring to a boil then lower to a simmer.

Add cilantro and chickpeas. Simmer for at least 45-60 minutes.

Serve over grain of choice.

Yield

6-8 *servings*

 GF

1 TSP	olive oil
8	celery stalks (about 2 cups), chopped
5	green onions, chopped
2 C	kale, chopped
1	parsnip, grated
2 C	fresh spinach, chopped
2 TSP	cumin
2 TSP	turmeric
2 TSP	sweet paprika
1	can organic tomato sauce (15 oz/425 g)
4 C	white butter beans, soaked overnight and drained
1 TSP	pure maple syrup
1/2 C	tricolor quinoa
1 TBSP	vegan sweet chili sauce
7-8 C	water
+	salt
+	pepper

Great comfort food that is loaded with iron and antioxidants.

Check out my tip on how to soak and cook beans (page 218).

BUTTER BEANS & QUINOA VEGGIE STEW

In a cast iron pot on medium heat, add olive oil, celery, green onions, salt and pepper. Sauté for a few minutes.

Add kale, parsnip, spinach, cumin, turmeric and sweet paprika. Continue to sauté for about 5-7 minutes, letting the flavors combine.

Add tomato sauce, beans, pure maple syrup, quinoa, sweet chili sauce and water. Bring to a boil, then lower heat to a simmer. Cook until the beans are soft and the sauce becomes nice and thick, about 45-55 minutes.

Serve over brown rice.

CHANTERELLE & PORTOBELLO MUSHROOM RAGOUT OVER RED LENTIL PURÉE

Yield

4-6 *servings*   GF

mushroom ragout:

1 TBSP	olive oil
1	medium onion, chopped
2	cloves garlic, chopped
1 LB	mixed mushrooms (chanterelle mushrooms, washed well and cut length-wise, and baby portobello mushrooms, washed and quartered)
1 TBSP	gluten-free oat flour
1/4 C	cognac
1 TSP	no beef base
1/2 TSP	agave
1/3 C	parsley, chopped
1/4 C	green onions, chopped
+	salt
+	pepper

for the lentils:

1 TSP	olive oil
1/2 C	onion, chopped
1	clove garlic, minced
1/4 TSP	yellow curry powder
1/4 TSP	turmeric
1 C	red lentils
2 C	water
+	salt
+	pepper

mushroom ragout:

In a large nonstick pan on medium heat, add olive oil, onion, salt and pepper. Sauté for a few minutes.

Add garlic and continue to sauté for a couple more minutes.

Add mushrooms. Sauté for a few minutes then sprinkle with gluten-free oat flour. Splash with cognac.

Add no beef base, agave, more salt and pepper. Keep mixing until the mushrooms get tender and the liquids start to evaporate.

Add parsley and chopped green onions. Mix well and remove from heat.

lentils:

In a small pot, add olive oil and chopped onion, sauté for a few minutes.

Add minced garlic, salt, pepper, curry, turmeric and lentils. Stir

continuously for a couple of minutes until you smell the aroma from the spices.

Add water and let simmer until the lentils break down to a purée-like texture.

serving suggestion:

Pour about a cup of the lentils into a large soup bowl. Top with a cup or more of the mushrooms in the center of the plate.

———————— ————————

Chanterelle mushrooms have a very meaty and earthy texture. I love using them in this ragout, as well as in soups. The cognac in this dish enhances all the flavors and ties them together.

———————— ⚕ ————————

Yield

10   *mini-pumpkins*

10   mini pumpkins, washed
     and dried
 +   olive oil
 +   salt
 +   pepper
 1   package couscous
     (about 1 1/2 cups dry
     couscous)
1 TSP no chicken base
1 1/2 C cooked garbanzo beans

BAKED MINI PUMPKIN WITH COUSCOUS & GARBANZO BEANS

Mini pumpkins bring any fall dish to the next level. As much as they are aesthetically pleasing, they are equally as delicious.

Check out my tip on how to soak and cook beans (page 218).

Heat oven to 375° F.

for the pumpkins:

Gently cut off the tops of the pumpkins, save, and set aside. Scoop out the seeds with a spoon and place the emptied pumpkins face up on a baking sheet.

Drizzle the inside of the pumpkins with olive oil, salt and pepper. Place the tops back on the pumpkins. Add approximately 1 cup of water to the baking sheet. Bake for about 15-20 minutes, until pumpkins are tender but still keep their shape.

couscous:

Cook the couscous according to the package's instructions. Mix in the cooked garbanzo beans, no chicken base, salt and pepper.

assembly:

Fill the pumpkins with the couscous mixture and bake for about 10-15 minutes, until the pumpkins are heated through. Serve warm.

Yield

8-10 *servings*

1 TSP	olive oil
1	onion, chopped
1	head of garlic, peeled and chopped
1 C	green lentils, soaked overnight and drained
1 C	garbanzo beans, soaked overnight and drained
3 C	dried cannellini beans, soaked overnight and drained
1/2 C	kidney beans, soaked overnight and drained
1/2 C	lima beans, soaked overnight and drained
1 1/2 C	pearl barley
3	yams, peeled and cut into cubes
1 TBSP	turmeric
1 TBSP	sweet paprika
1 TBSP	Old Bay Seasoning
1 TBSP	pure maple syrup
1 TBSP	no chicken base
8 C	water
+	salt
+	pepper

Tshulent is the most common stew in the Jewish kitchen. It is tradition not to cook on the Sabbath, so the stew is prepared on Friday evening and left to simmer overnight.

Growing up, my mom used to make tshulent on our wood stove during the winter season. I remember the smell in the house was so strong and tempting that it was hard to wait until lunch time. I recreated this favorite stew of mine in vegan form, and the results are outstanding.

Check out my tip on how to soak and cook beans (page 218).

TSHULENT

In a large pot, add olive oil, onion, salt and pepper. Sauté for a few minutes on medium heat.

Then add garlic and lentils. Sauté for about 5-7 minutes more.

Add beans, pearl barley, yams, all seasonings and water. Bring to a boil and then reduce heat to a simmer. Cook for about 1/2 hour, then pour into a crock pot and cook on low heat for about 8-10 hours.

Serve warm.

Yield

4-6 *servings*

3 TSP	olive oil
2 C	leeks, chopped
3 TSP	shawarma spice blend
2 C	green lentils
1 TSP	agave
4 C	water
+	salt
+	pepper

SHAWARMA-SPICED LENTILS

I love shawarma spices. Their richness makes the whole dish. This meal is super easy to make and the spices create a sophisticated, distinctly flavored dish. Great as a side dish or as a main course over brown rice.

Leeks always carry dirt, therefore, they need to be soaked. You want to slice into rings first, then separate and place into a large bowl of water. Next, dry in a salad spinner or with a dry towel.

In a nonstick saucepan on medium heat, add olive oil, leeks, salt, pepper and shawarma spices. Sauté for a few minutes.

Add the lentils, agave and more salt and pepper. Sauté for a couple more minutes.

Add water. Bring to a boil then lower to a simmer with the lid on for about 40-50 minutes, until the lentils are tender and the sauce has thickened.

Serve over brown rice.

Yield

4-6 *servings*

1 TBSP	olive oil
1	large onion, thinly chopped
1	large clove of garlic, minced
2 C	spelt
1 C	black lentils
4 C	water
+	salt
+	pepper

SPELT & BLACK LENTIL MAJADRA

Without compromising the flavor, I added more nutrition to this dish by using spelt instead of traditional rice. The texture is very crunchy and unique. I personally enjoy the distinct combination of texture and flavors that this dish brings out. It is pure health on a plate.

This dish can easily be transformed into gluten free by substituting the spelt with brown rice.

In a wide saucepan on medium heat, add olive oil, onion, salt and pepper. Sauté for a couple of minutes.

Add minced garlic and sauté for a couple more minutes.

Add spelt and lentils and keep sautéing for about 2 minutes.

Add water and bring to a boil. Lower heat to a simmer and cook for about 1 hour or until the spelt has absorbed all the water.

Serve warm.

Yield

6-8 *servings*

2 TBSP	olive oil, divided
1	onion, chopped
4 C	fresh mushrooms, sliced
1 1/4 C	brown rice
3 TBSP	gf low sodium soy sauce
2 1/2 C	water
+	salt
+	pepper

BAKED BROWN RICE WITH MUSHROOMS

Baked rice is a dish I grew up with. My mom used to make it often, and it was a hit every single time. My mom wasn't big on rice—she was more of a potato lover—but this is one of her go-to rice dishes that we all loved so much.

Heat oven to 375° F.

In a nonstick pan on medium heat, add 1 tablespoon olive oil, onion, salt and pepper. Sauté for a few minutes, then add mushrooms and keep mixing until golden.

In a 9" x 12" Pyrex dish, add the mushroom mixture, rice, soy sauce, water, pepper and 1 tablespoon olive oil. Cover with aluminum foil and bake for about 1 hour or until all the water has been absorbed by the rice.

Remove the aluminum foil and broil for a couple of minutes until golden brown and crunchy.

Serve warm.

Yield

4-6 *servings*

 GF

1 TBSP	coconut oil
2 C	onions, thinly chopped
3	celery stalks, thinly chopped
3	cloves garlic, minced
1 TBSP	fresh ginger, grated
1 TSP	garam masala
1 TSP	cumin seeds
1/2 TSP	ground coriander
1 TSP	turmeric
1 C	red lentils, washed and drained
1 C	azuki beans, soaked overnight and drained
1	can of organic diced tomatoes (14.5 oz/411 g)
2-3 C	water
3 TBSP	tamari
+	salt
+	pepper

rice:

2 C	brown rice
1 TBSP	olive oil
4 C	water
+	salt

Indian food is one of my favorite cuisines. I can't get enough of it! Did you know that the spices used in Indian food are medicinal? Each spice has its own benefit.

Dahl is a great dish packed with protein and a combination of fresh and dry spices.

Check out my tip on how to soak and cook beans (page 218).

INDIAN RED LENTIL & AZUKI DAHL OVER BROWN RICE

In a cast iron skillet on medium heat, add coconut oil, onions, celery, salt and pepper. Sauté for a few minutes.

Then add garlic, ginger, garam masala, cumin seeds, coriander and turmeric. Continue to sauté spices until fragrant.

Add the lentils, azuki, diced tomatoes, water and tamari. Lower the heat to a simmer and cook until the beans and lentils are completely tender. If you like your dahl more liquidy, add more water. I added just 2 cups of water, but you can certainly add more to create a consistency to your liking.

rice:

In a pot on medium heat, add olive oil and rice. Stir for a few minutes. Add water and salt. Bring to a boil, then lower to a simmer until the rice has absorbed all the water.

ARTICHOKE HEARTS, VEGGIES & BROWN RICE DELIGHT

Yield

4-6 *servings*

 (GF)

eggplants:

- 3 medium eggplants
- + olive oil spray
- + salt
- + pepper

rice mixture:

1 TBSP	olive oil
1	medium onion, chopped
1	clove of garlic, minced
2	celery stalks, thinly sliced
2	carrots, thinly cubed
1	package steamed artichoke hearts, quartered (12.68 oz/360 g)
1 C	brown rice
2 C	boiling water
1 TSP	vegetable base
2	green onions, sliced
+	salt
+	pepper

Brown rice is definitely a much wiser choice over regular rice. Since it is the unrefined version of white rice, it is loaded with beneficial vitamins that reduce the risk of developing certain illnesses, and naturally occurring oils that help balance cholesterol levels.

The fiber in brown rice also promotes weight loss.

Heat oven to 375° F.

Take a baking sheet and line with parchment paper.

Cut the eggplants into small cubes.

Lay on a baking sheet, sprinkle with salt and pepper, then spray with olive oil. Bake until golden brown and tender, about 20 minutes. Set aside.

In a large pot on medium heat, add olive oil, onion, salt and pepper. Sauté for about 4 minutes.

Add garlic, celery and carrots. Sauté for 5 more minutes.

Add artichoke hearts and rice. Sauté for a couple of minutes.

Add water and vegetable base. Bring to a boil then lower heat to a simmer and allow the rice to absorb all the water, about 30 minutes.

Add eggplant and green onions, mix to combine, and serve.

Yield

4-6 *servings*

1 TSP	coconut oil
+	organic sprouted tofu extra firm (15.5 oz/439 g), cut into cubes
1 1/2 TBSP	olive oil
2	leeks (6 oz/170 g), thinly chopped
+	salt
+	pepper
1 TBSP	fresh turmeric root, grated
1 TSP	fresh ginger root, grated
1 TBSP	ground coriander
1	package of artichoke hearts (8 oz/226 g), frozen and thawed
3 C	organic frozen sweet baby peas
2 1/4 C	water
1 TSP	vegetable base
1 C	fresh chopped cilantro

Growing up, my mom never used cilantro in her cooking. She only used parsley, the European way. After moving to the U.S., I was exposed to a lot of cilantro in Mexican food, and now I love it.

In this recipe, the cilantro is the main component that binds the flavors together. Another great ingredient in this dish is fresh turmeric root, which colors the dish nicely and adds many health benefits. It has anti-inflammatory properties and antioxidants, which help prevent cancer.

Refer to the tip on how to wash leeks (page 64).

MEDITERRANEAN TOFU BOWL

In a nonstick pan on medium heat, add coconut oil and cubed tofu. Sauté the tofu until golden and crunchy. Sprinkle with salt. Set aside.

In a large cast iron pan, add olive oil, leeks, salt and pepper. Sauté on medium heat until translucent.

Add the turmeric, ginger and coriander. Lower heat and sauté for another minute.

Add artichoke hearts and sweet peas. Sauté for a couple more minutes.

Add water and vegetable base. Bring to a boil then lower to a simmer. Cook for about 20 minutes.

Add chopped cilantro and cook for 5-10 more minutes.

Add tofu, mix and serve.

Yield

4-6 *servings*

1 TSP	olive oil
1	large onion, chopped
2	cloves garlic, minced
1 1/2 C	organic corn
1	large yam, cut into cubes
1 C	garbanzo beans, soaked overnight, cooked and drained
1 1/2 C	cooked red beans
1 TBSP	curry powder
1	can light coconut milk (13.66 oz/403 g)
+	salt
+	pepper

COLORFUL VEGGIE CURRY BOWL

There is something about the combination of yellow curry and coconut milk that is so comforting.

The freshness of the vegetables, the smoothness of the beans, and the vibrant aroma of warm spices make this dish loved by everyone. The nice thing about it: it's so easy and quick to make. In no time, you have a healthy, satisfying and delicious dinner on the table.

Check out my tip on how to soak and cook beans (page 218).

In a large nonstick pan on medium heat, add olive oil and onion, salt and pepper. Sauté until translucent.

Add garlic. Sauté for a couple more minutes.

Add corn, yam, garbanzo beans, red beans, and curry powder. Sauté for a couple more minutes.

Add coconut milk. Lower heat to a simmer and let cook for at least 30-40 minutes, until all the flavors have combined.

Serve over brown rice (page 128).

4-6 *servings*

 GF

1 package soy curls (8 oz/227 g), soaked in lukewarm water for 10-15 minutes then drained
1 TBSP olive oil
4 TBSP tomato paste
2 TBSP homemade chili garlic base (see page 47)
1 TSP fresh ginger root, grated
1 TSP fresh turmeric root, grated
1 large yam, grated
1 red bell pepper, thinly chopped
1 jalapeño pepper, thinly chopped
1 TBSP vegetable base
1 can organic tomato sauce (15 oz/425 g)
1 1/2 C water
1 C fresh cilantro, chopped
+ salt
+ pepper

Chraime is a traditional fish dish prepared in many Tripolitan kitchens. I love this dish, so I created a sauce using chraime's secret ingredients, but instead of fish I use soy curls. It is a very flavorful and spicy dish that is easy to make, even for large groups.

Serve over rice or quinoa. Feel free to vary the amount of spices to your liking.

SPICY SOY CURL CHRAIME

Heat oven to 375° F.

In a large cast iron skillet on medium heat, add olive oil, tomato paste and homemade chili garlic base. With a whisk, mix for a few minutes until fragrant.

Add ginger, turmeric, grated yam, salt and pepper. Sauté for a few minutes, stirring constantly.

Add red pepper, jalapeño, vegetable base, tomato sauce and water. Mix well. Bring to a boil then lower heat to a simmer.

Add the soaked and drained soy curls and cilantro. Let cook for 30-40 minutes. Mix from time to time. The sauce should be thick.

Serve with a good rustic bread to dip in the sauce.

STUFFED CHARD LEAVES

Yield

6-8 *servings*   GF

---

rice:

1 C black or brown rice
2 C water
 +   salt
 1   package sun dried
     tomatoes (3.5 oz/100 g),
     chopped, divided
1/2 C sautéed onions
 4   Brazil nuts, chopped

chard:

 1   bunch fresh chard leaves
     (about 15 leaves)

sauce:

1 C   coconut water
1 TSP vegetable base
1 TSP gf organic mellow white
      miso
 +   salt
 +   pepper
1/2 C water

topping:

 +   olive oil

for the rice:

Add rice to a sauce pan along with water, salt, and 3/4 of the chopped sun dried tomatoes. Cook on low heat until the water has evaporated. Add sautéed onions and Brazil nuts. Mix and set aside.

for the chard:

Cut away the thick parts of the stems—starting from the bottom of each leaf, cut up to the center of the leaf and back down again in an upside down "V" shape. Chop the stems and add both the stems and the remaining 1/4 of the sun dried tomatoes to a large nonstick pan. (Create a bed for the stuffed leaves.)

for the sauce:

In a mixing bowl, whisk 1 cup coconut water, vegetable base, white miso, salt, pepper, and 1/2 cup water. Set aside.

preparation:

Lay one leaf on a working surface with the bottom facing you. Add about 2 tablespoons of the rice stuffing to the center of the leaf. First, fold the sides of the leaf to the center. Then tightly roll the leaf from the bottom to the top. Place the stuffed leaf, seam-side down on a bed of chopped stems and sun dried tomatoes.

Do the same for all of the leaves and place them tightly together in the pan.

Pour the sauce over the stuffed leaves and cook on low heat for about 1/2 an hour.

Drizzle with extra virgin olive oil and serve warm.

Tamales are a great food to make ahead of time and freeze for later. When your kids get hungry and you don't have time to cook, simply warm them up in the oven or in the microwave and enjoy.

I must admit that tamales take a long time to make, so if you don't have the time, don't get yourself into it. On the other hand, I think that the process is well worth it! This recipe is light in fat and loaded with nutrition. Beans, veggies, spices—such a flavorful dish! Don't substitute the masa flour with any other corn flour because it won't end up the same. The masa flour gives them that special tamale flavor.

Check out my tip on how to soak and cook beans (page 218).

Yield

4-6 *servings*

 GF

+ olive oil
1 eggplant, sliced
1 yam, sliced
1 large onion, sliced
+ salt
+ pepper

polenta

2 C water
1 TSP salt
1 TBSP olive oil
1/2 C polenta

topping:

+ olive oil

Roasted vegetables are a great way to eat your daily vegetables. Simplicity is key in this recipe. Salt, pepper and some good olive oil work like magic. You can always add more flavor by drizzling the tower with tahini sauce (page 46), which is loaded with protein and vitamins. Great as a side dish or as a main dish.

ROASTED TOWER

Heat oven to 375° F.

Line a baking sheet with parchment paper and drizzle with olive oil. Spread out the eggplant, yams and onions evenly on the baking sheet. Drizzle with olive oil and sprinkle with salt and pepper.

Bake for about 20 minutes, then flip to the other side and cook for a few more minutes until golden brown. Set aside.

polenta:

In a saucepan, add water and bring to a boil. Add 1 teaspoon salt, olive oil and polenta, then reduce heat to low. Stir constantly until thick and the water has been absorbed.

Pour the mixture onto a baking sheet lined with parchment paper and smooth into an even layer with a spatula. Try to match the thickness of the polenta to the thickness of the eggplant, yam and onion slices. Let the polenta sit until it is cool and firm. Take a round cookie cutter and cut circles.

assembly:

Tower your ingredients one on top of one another. Drizzle with olive oil and serve warm.

GF

2 TBSP   olive oil, divided
     1   onion, sliced
2 TBSP   shawarma spices
     1   package dried soy curls
         (8 oz/227 g), soaked in
         lukewarm water for 10-
         15 minutes and drained
1 TSP   agave
     +   salt
     +   pepper

SOY CURLS SHAWARMA

Shawarma is a classic Mediterranean dish that is loaded with spices and kick. There is just something about the flavor that makes it the perfect comfort food. Shawarma spices can be purchased at any Mediterranean grocery store or online. The best way to serve shawarma is in a pita pocket with hummus, tahini, pickles and Israeli salad.

In a nonstick pan on medium heat, add 1 tablespoon olive oil, onion, salt and pepper. Sauté for a few minutes until translucent.

Add shawarma spices and continue to cook for about one minute.

Add soy curls and agave. Keep mixing on low heat until all the flavors have incorporated evenly, about 15 minutes. Add another tablespoon of olive oil and serve warm. You can serve in warm pita bread and drizzle with tahini sauce (page 46).

MUSHROOM KIBBEH

Yield

30 *kibbeh*

dough:

2 C	bulgur
2 1/2 C	boiling water
2 C	garbanzo bean flour
2 TBSP	olive oil
+	salt
+	pepper

filling:

1 TBSP	olive oil
2	small onions, chopped
1	clove garlic, minced
8 OZ	organic crimini mushrooms, chopped
8 OZ	organic white mushrooms, chopped
+	salt
+	pepper

sauce / soup:

1 TBSP	olive oil
1	large leek, thinly chopped
10	mini carrots, chopped
1 TSP	fresh ginger, grated
2	small red bell peppers, thinly chopped
1	jalapeño pepper, seeded and chopped
1 TBSP	Old Bay Seasoning
1 TBSP	sweet paprika
1 TBSP	pure maple syrup
1 TBSP	organic white miso paste
4 C	water
+	salt
+	pepper

dough:

In a mixing bowl, add bulgur, salt and boiling water. Cover and let sit for about 15 minutes. Then add garbanzo bean flour and olive oil. Mix with your hands to create a dough, cover, and let sit for about 45 minutes.

filling:

Heat olive oil in a pan on medium heat, add chopped onions, garlic, salt and pepper. Sauté for about 2-3 minutes, then add mushrooms, and a bit more salt and pepper. Sauté until all the liquids have evaporated and the mushrooms are tender. Let cool and set aside.

sauce:

Heat one tablespoon olive oil in a large, deep pan on medium heat. Add chopped leek and carrots and sauté for about 5 minutes.

Add ginger, red bell peppers, jalapeño, salt and pepper. Sauté for about 5 minutes.

Add Old Bay Seasoning, paprika, pure maple syrup and miso paste. Sauté for 1 more minute, while mixing constantly. You can slowly add some of the water to help free any bits that have stuck to the bottom of the pan.

Add remaining water. Cover and lower to a simmer. Cook for at least 30 minutes.

kibbeh:

Scoop about 1 tablespoon of dough into a ball. Wet your hands and flatten into a circle. Add about one tablespoon of mushroom filling to the center. Gently close the sides of the dough into a ball again.

Assemble all the kibbeh balls and add them to the sauce pan. Simmer for 30-40 minutes. Shake the pan from time to time so that the sauce covers the balls and they absorb the flavors.

---------------- ----------------

Kibbeh is one of my favorite Middle Eastern dishes. Kibbeh is originally filled with ground beef and cooked in beet or butternut squash soup. Although this recipe is somewhat complex, it is well worth the time put into it, especially if you make a large quantity and freeze some for later. The sauce I originally made had two jalepeños and was a bit too spicy for my kids. If you like heat, then add another jalapeño. If you like just a little heat, stick to the recipe or remove jalapeño for a mild dish.

---------------- ----------------

Yield

6-8 *servings*

(GF)

6	small yams, cut lengthwise in half
I TBSP	olive oil
+	salt
+	pepper
I TSP	olive oil
2	small yams, peeled and chopped in the food processor
I	green onion, chopped
I	clove of garlic, minced
+	salt
+	pepper

filling:

1/4 C	brown rice
1/4 C	green lentils
I C	water
+	salt
+	pepper
+	chopped parsley for serving

Yams are loaded with vitamins such as B-complex and vitamin C. They contain potassium, copper and iron as well as fiber that helps digestion. Yams are carbohydrates but have a low glycemic index, meaning they don't quickly raise then drop your blood sugar. Combining yams with more fiber and complex carbohydrates, such as brown rice, creates a satisfying meal with a delicious sweet and savory flavor.

LENTIL STUFFED YAMS

Heat oven to 375° F.

Line a baking sheet with parchment paper then drizzle with olive oil and sprinkle with salt and pepper. Lay the halved yams face down on the baking sheet.

Bake for about 20 minutes or until tender.

While you're waiting, heat olive oil in a nonstick pan on medium heat and sauté the chopped yams with green onion, garlic, salt and pepper. Set aside.

filling:

In a sauce pan, add rice, lentils, water and salt. Bring to a boil, then lower to a simmer. Cook until the rice and the lentils have absorbed all the water.

assemble the dish:

Make a cut down the center of the halved yams. With the back of a spoon, gently push into the slits to create a little oval, bathtub-like shape. Then fill the yams with the brown rice and lentil mixture. Sprinkle with the sautéed yam and chopped parsley. Drizzle with olive oil, and sprinkle with salt and pepper. Serve.

Yield

12 *tacos*

1 package of 12 yellow corn taco shells
1 TBSP olive oil
2 TSP shawarma spices
14 OZ extra firm tofu, cubed
2 C kidney beans, soaked overnight, cooked and drained
3 carrots (red, yellow and white), chopped in a food processor
2 tomatoes, cubed
2 avocados, sliced
1 bunch of cilantro, chopped
1 head of lettuce, chopped
2 C arugula
2 green onions, chopped
+ salt
+ pepper

Top with your favorite salsa and guacamole.

Check out my tip on how to soak and cook beans (page 218).

TACOS

shawarma spiced tofu:

In a nonstick pan on medium-low heat, add olive oil and shawarma spices. Heat for 1 minute. Be careful not to burn the spices.

Add tofu and sauté until golden brown, about 15 minutes or so.

Sprinkle with salt and pepper. Set aside.

assemble the tacos:

Take one taco shell and fill with lettuce and arugula, then add beans, tofu, tomatoes, and avocado. Garnish with chopped carrots, cilantro and green onion.

Yield

6-8 *servings*

 GF

cauliflower puree:

2 LB	cauliflower, cut into florets
1 TBSP	olive oil
1 TSP	Old Bay Seasoning
+	salt + pepper

pie filling:

1 TBSP	olive oil
1	leek, chopped (about 1 cup)
2	cloves garlic, minced
1 C	TVP, soaked in 1 cup boiling water, salt, pepper
1	carrot, cubed
1 C	frozen peas, thawed
1 C	frozen corn, thawed
1 C	pinto beans, soaked overnight and drained
3	celery stalks, cubed
1	can organic diced tomatoes (14.5 oz/411 g)
1 TBSP	Old Bay Seasoning
1 TBSP	tomato paste
2 C	boiling water
+	salt
+	pepper

Shepherd's pie tastes even better the next day. The flavors blend and soak into the veggies and TVP. Non-vegan guests may even mistake it for ground meat because the texture is so similar.

The trick is to cut calories by adding more veggies and using cauliflower instead of potatoes.

Check out my tip on how to soak and cook beans (page 218).

SHEPHERD'S PIE TOPPED WITH CAULIFLOWER PURÉE

Heat oven to 350° F.

To a pot, add the cauliflower florets. Cover with water and add a teaspoon of salt. Cook on high heat until tender, about 15 minutes.

Drain and blend the cauliflower, olive oil and Old Bay Seasoning using a hand blender until creamy. Set aside.

In a cast iron skillet, add olive oil, leek, garlic, salt and pepper. Sauté on medium heat for about 5 minutes.

Add TVP, carrots, peas, corn, pinto beans, celery stalks, tomatoes, and Old Bay Seasoning. Sauté for about 10-15 minutes.

Add tomato paste and boiling water. Bring to a boil then reduce heat to low and cook for about 30 minutes.

Pour the mixture into a pyrex dish, top with the cauliflower purée, cover with aluminum foil and bake for about 45 minutes. Remove foil, let set for about 10 minutes and serve.

Yield

4 *slices*

quinoa crust:

1 C	quinoa, soaked overnight with plenty of water and drained
1 TSP	baking powder
1/4 C	water
+	salt
+	pepper
1 TSP	olive oil for pan

roasted veggies:

1	red bell pepper, sliced
1	portobello mushroom, sliced
1	onion, sliced
+	olive oil
+	salt
+	pepper

spread:

| 2 TBSP | basil pesto or spinach pesto (recipe on page 159) |

If you like your crust thin, divide the batter into 2 crusts. You can also bake the crust in the oven on a baking sheet, lined with parchment paper and greased with olive oil. It will cook pretty quickly and should look pale but completely cooked (like a pancake), about 15 minutes. Then spread the pesto while it's hot, and lay the veggies. You can bake it again for 5-10 minutes to warm through.

QUINOA CRUST ROASTED VEGGIE PIZZA

Turn oven to broil.

In a food processor, add drained quinoa, baking powder, water, salt and pepper. Blend until smooth. Set aside.

Place sliced vegetables on a baking sheet lined with parchment paper. Drizzle with olive oil, salt and pepper. Broil for a few minutes on each side until golden brown. Set aside.

In a nonstick pan on low heat, heat olive oil then add quinoa batter. Cook for about 5-7 minutes until edges are golden

brown. Finish in the oven under the broiler, or flip crust to the other side for 2 minutes (until golden brown).

Remove from oven and while still hot, spread the pesto on top (this makes it melt into the crust).

Top with veggies and serve immediately.

STUFFED EGGPLANT

Yield

6-8 *servings*

eggplant:

3   eggplants, sliced lengthwise (about 1/2" thick)
+   olive oil
+   salt
+   pepper

stuffing:

1 C   green lentils
2 1/2 C   water
1 TSP   olive oil
1   large onion, chopped
2 C   fresh mushrooms, sliced
3 C   fresh spinach, chopped
+   salt
+   pepper

sauce:

1   jar of marinara sauce (2 lb/907 g)

Heat oven to 375° F.

Line a baking sheet with parchment paper and drizzle with olive oil. Place the eggplant slices on the baking sheet and drizzle with olive oil. Sprinkle with salt and pepper and bake for about 20-25 minutes, until golden brown and tender. Set aside.

To a sauce pot, add lentils, water and salt. Bring to a boil then reduce heat to low. Cook until the lentils have absorbed all the water. Set aside.

In a nonstick pan on medium heat, add olive oil, onions, salt and pepper. Sauté for a few minutes.

Add mushrooms and a bit more salt and pepper. Sauté for about 10 more minutes.

Add spinach and cook for 3 more minutes. Add cooked lentils, mix and remove from heat.

assemble the dish:

Lay one slice of eggplant on a working surface. Spread a spoonful or more of filling in the center of the eggplant, roll it up, then place seam-side down in a large Pyrex dish. Repeat with the other eggplants, top evenly with marinara sauce and bake for about 35-45 minutes.

Let cool slightly before serving.

Yield

4-6 *servings*

2 TSP olive oil
1 large onion, sliced
2 cloves garlic, minced
1 TSP ginger, minced
3 C broccoli (fresh or frozen and thawed)
1 TBSP coconut oil
1 package sprouted organic tofu (15.5 oz/439 g)
3 C fresh shishito peppers
1 TBSP gf soy sauce/tamari
1 TBSP vegan sweet chili sauce
✦ salt
✦ pepper

SHISHITO PEPPERS OVER CRUNCHY TOFU & BROCCOLI

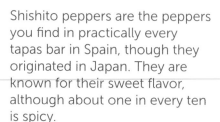

Shishito peppers are the peppers you find in practically every tapas bar in Spain, though they originated in Japan. They are known for their sweet flavor, although about one in every ten is spicy.

Peppers generally are low-calorie, loaded with vitamins such as C and K, and often offer anti-inflammatory properties.

In a large nonstick pan on medium heat, add olive oil, onion, salt and pepper. Sauté until translucent. Add garlic and ginger, and sauté for another minute or so. Add broccoli and lower heat to a simmer.

In another nonstick pan on medium heat, add the coconut oil, tofu, salt and pepper. Sauté one side until golden, flip, then sauté the other side until golden. Be gentle not to break the tofu.

Add the tofu to the broccoli-onion pan. Then add the shishito peppers, soy sauce, sweet chili

sauce, and more salt and pepper. Let simmer until the peppers are nice and tender, but not mushy, and all the flavors have combined.

Serve immediately.

Yield

3-4 *servings*

1	can light coconut milk (13.5 oz/400 ml)
1 1/2 TBSP	vegan red curry paste
1 TSP	vegan sweet chili sauce
1 TSP	fresh ginger, grated
1	eggplant, cubed
1	jalapeño, sliced
+	salt
+	pepper

SPICY EGGPLANT CURRY

You can use this same curry sauce with your favorite vegetables like green beans, Brussels sprouts, cauliflower, or broccoli. You don't have to limit yourself to just eggplant. Be creative.

In a nonstick pan on medium heat, add coconut milk, red curry paste, sweet chili sauce, fresh ginger, salt and pepper. Bring to a boil then reduce heat to low.

Add eggplant and jalapeño.

Cover with lid and let simmer for about 30-40 minutes.

Serve warm over brown rice.

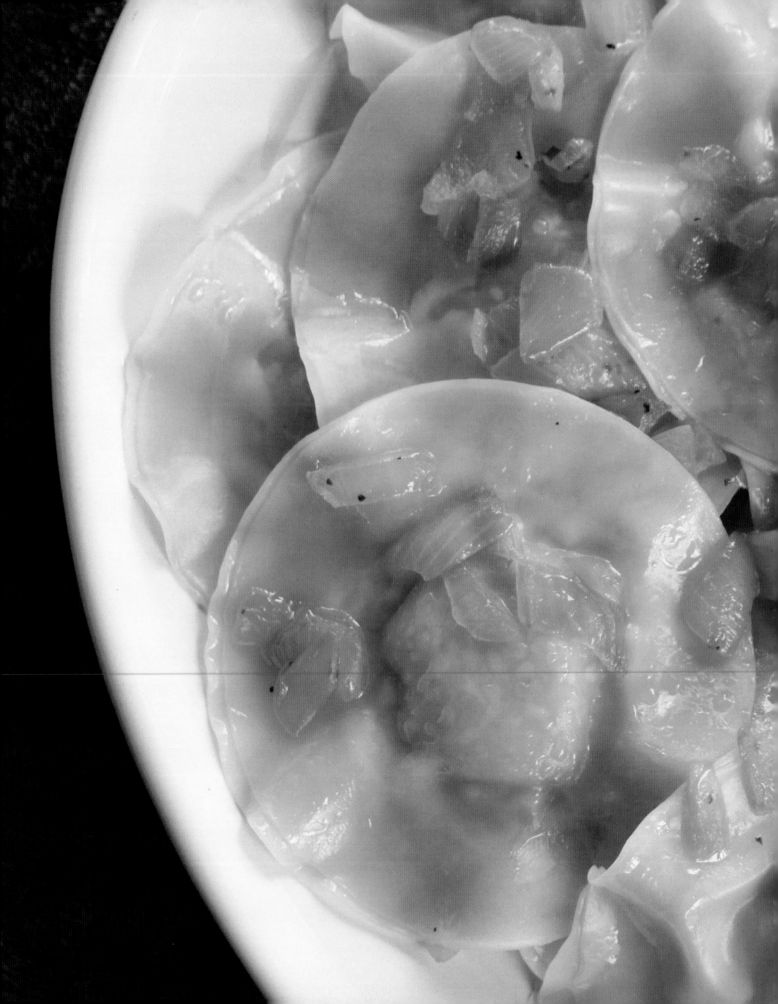

Pasta

ZUCCHINI SPAGHETTI

Yield

4-6 *servings*

1	package gluten-free brown rice spaghetti (1 lb/454 g)
6	zucchinis, spiralized
1 TBSP	olive oil
2	cloves garlic, minced
+	salt
+	pepper

for serving:

+ parsley

Cook the pasta according to package directions.

In a large pan on medium-low heat, add olive oil and garlic. Sauté for a minute, stirring constantly. (Be careful not to burn the garlic.)

Add zucchini, salt and pepper. Toss in the pan to heat through. Add cooked pasta, mix well and serve.

Drizzle with olive oil and garnish with parsley.

Although this process may be a bit time-consuming, you can do it in stages. Prepare the cheese even a couple of days in advance, and roast the vegetables the day before. Then, all you need to do is assemble the lasagna and bake.

Yield

4-6 *servings*

1/2 C	raw cashews, soaked overnight and drained
1	clove garlic
3 C	fresh baby spinach
+	salt
+	pepper
1/4 C	olive oil or less
+	cooked pasta (16oz/454g)

SPINACH PESTO PASTA

Spinach is a great way to consume your daily requirements of iron and antioxidants.

Tip: you can use that pesto sauce on the quinoa crust roasted veggie pizza (page 146)

In a food processor, add cashews, garlic, spinach, salt and pepper.

Start blending then slowly pour in the olive oil so that it can incorporate properly.

Pour the sauce over the pasta and serve.

4-6 *servings*

 GF

- 5 medium/large parsnips, peeled
- 1 clove of garlic, peeled
- 1 TBSP olive oil
- 1 can light coconut milk (14 oz/400 ml)
- + salt
- + pepper
- + cooked gluten-free brown rice pasta or other pasta of your choice (16 oz/454 g)

topping:

- + olive oil

Parsnips are similar to carrots only sweeter and the flavor is more distinct. Parsnips are an excellent source of fiber and antioxidants. They are also known to be anti-inflammatory and rich in vitamins (such as vitamin C, B, and folic acid) and minerals (such as iron, calcium and potassium).

I personally love to add root vegetables to many of my recipes, not only because of their high nutritional value, but also because of their amazing, earthy flavors.

CREAMY PARSNIP PASTA

In a food processor, add parsnip and garlic. Mix until you reach a rice texture.

In a nonstick pan on medium heat, add olive oil, parsnip-garlic mixture, salt and pepper. Sauté for a few minutes, stirring constantly.

Add coconut milk and lower to a simmer. Cook for about 20-30 minutes until the sauce becomes soft and creamy.

Pour over pasta, drizzle with a little olive oil and serve.

YAM GNOCCHI IN ALMOND SAGE SAUCE

Yield

4-6 *servings*

for the gnocchi:

1	large yam, cooked, drained and mashed
1/2 C	semolina flour
1/2 C	spelt flour
1 TBSP	flaxseed meal
+	salt
+	pepper

sauté ingredients:

1-2 TBSP	olive oil
10	fresh sage leaves

sauce:

1 TBSP	olive oil
1	onion, chopped
1	clove of garlic, minced
1 C	slivered almonds, soaked for 2-3 hours and drained
1 TSP	vegetable base
1 C	boiling water
+	salt
+	pepper

for the gnocchi:

In a bowl, add all ingredients and mix well.

Cool in the refrigerator for one hour.

Portion evenly sized gnocchi with a spoon, hand-roll into small-sized balls and press with a fork to create indentations.

tip:

Wet the spoon, fork, and your hands during the process to prevent sticking.

Bring a large pot of salty water to a boil.

Very gently add the gnocchi to the boiling water. As soon as the gnocchi begin to float, transfer to a plate with a slotted spoon. Make sure you don't put one on top of the other or they may stick to one another.

Heat 1-2 tablespoons olive oil in a nonstick pan on medium heat. Add the sage leaves and the gnocchi in batches. Don't overcrowd the pan and be very gentle not to break the gnocchi.

Sauté each side just until golden (it happens pretty quickly). Set aside.

sauce:

In a nonstick pan on medium heat, add olive oil, onion, garlic, salt and pepper. Sauté until tender.

Next, add to a food processor: almonds, sautéed onions, vegetable base, water, salt, pepper, and the sage leaves from the sauté pan.

Blend until very smooth.

Pour the sauce back into the pan and heat.

to serve:

Pour sauce onto a plate, top with gnocchi, garnish with sage leaves.

Yield

24	*kreplach*

1 TBSP	olive oil
2	medium onions, chopped
2	sweet or regular potatoes, cooked, peeled and puréed
1	package gyoza wrappers (12 oz/340 g)
+	salt
+	pepper

topping:

+	olive oil

Kreplach were one of my childhood treats made by my grandma and mom. They are basically the "ravioli" of the Eastern European kitchen.

Their smell brings back so many memories of celebrations and special occasions. Usually we only had them for special Shabbat dinners or holidays, since back then the dough was made by hand, so was quite the job to make from scratch.

These days you can find gyoza wrappers in most supermarkets. They work perfectly.

Tip: if you want to keep it traditional, you can use one gyoza wrapper per kreplach by forming a half moon shape and then you will double your batch of kreplach.

KREPLACH

In a nonstick pan, add olive oil and onions. Sauté on medium heat until golden.

Mix the sweet potatoes with half of the sautéed onions and set aside.

Bring a large pot of water to a boil. Add some salt.

assemble:

Prepare a bowl of water to dip your fingers in.

Place a spoonful of filling in the center of the wrapper. Dip your finger in the water and wet the outside edge of the wrapper. This will make the wrapper sticky and act like glue.

Lay another wrapper on top and press the top and bottom wrapper edges together tightly. Lay on parchment paper.

Repeat the same steps with the remaining wraps and filling. You should end up with about 24 kreplach.

In the boiling water, start adding 3-4 kreplach at a time. Cook until they start to float then move to a serving plate with a slotted spoon. Be careful not to place them on top of one another or they will stick together.

Top with sautéed onion, drizzle with olive oil and serve.

Yield

4-6 *servings*

1 TBSP   coconut oil

3   red bell peppers, cut into thin strips

4   celery stalks, cut into thin strips

1   package mixed, dried wild mushrooms (88 oz/25 g), soaked in warm water for 10 minutes and drained

1 1/2 TBSP   fresh ginger, grated

3   cloves garlic, thinly chopped

3   large green onions, chopped

sauce:

1 TSP   gf red miso paste

3 TBSP   coconut water

2 TBSP   vegan sweet chili sauce

+   salt

+   pepper

noodles:

1   package japanese soba noodles, gluten-free buckwheat (9.5 oz/269 g)

Stir fry is another great way to eat your veggies. Cooking time on high heat is quick, and the vegetables stay firm, crunchy, and keep their nutrition. You can use whichever veggies you like or have on hand. To keep the meal more nutritious, I used buckwheat noodles. They are super mild in flavor and delicious.

STIR FRY VEGGIES OVER BUCKWHEAT NOODLES

Mix all sauce ingredients in a bowl using a whisk.

In a large nonstick pan, heat coconut oil on high heat. Add peppers, celery and mushrooms. Stir for a few minutes then add ginger and garlic. Continue to sauté for a few more minutes.

Add the sauce to the pan. It should sizzle and that's what you want. Lower the heat, add onions and mix for one minute. Set aside.

noodles:

Cook according to package instructions.

serving:

Place noodles in a bowl, top with stir fried veggies and serve immediately.

Desserts

Yield

8-10 *servings*

1 1/4 C	spelt flour
1/4 C	almond meal
1 TSP	flaxseed meal
1 TSP	baking soda
1 TSP	baking powder
1/2 TSP	cinnamon
1/4 TSP	salt
1/4 C	almond milk
3	mashed bananas
1/4 C	pure maple syrup
1/4 C	coconut oil
1/2 C	vegan dark chocolate chunks
+	powdered sugar

There are so many other ways to sweeten dishes rather than using cane sugar. For this banana bread, I used maple syrup to enhance the natural sweetness of the bananas.

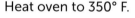

CHOCOLATE BANANA BREAD

Heat oven to 350° F.

Grease a loaf pan with coconut oil.

Excluding the chocolate chips, mix all dry ingredients (spelt flour, almond meal, flaxseed meal, baking powder, baking soda, cinnamon, salt) in a bowl.

Mix all the wet ingredients (almond milk, bananas, pure maple syrup, coconut oil) in another bowl using a whisk.

Pour the dry ingredients slowly into the wet ingredients and mix until combined. Fold in the chocolate chunks and pour mixture into the loaf pan.

Bake for about 40-50 minutes, until golden brown and completely set. You can check if it's done by inserting a toothpick into the loaf. If it comes out clean and dry, it's ready.

Let it cool for about 20 minutes.

Sprinkle with powdered sugar and serve.

Yield

7 *apples*

 GF

7	green apples, cored
3/4 C	raw pecans, chopped
3/4 C	gf quick cooking oats
1 TBSP	cinnamon
1 TBSP	vanilla sugar
1 C	red wine

BAKED GREEN APPLES

Baked apples make a home smell so warm and inviting. The smell of the cinnamon and the vanilla make you want to eat the whole dish yourself. The good thing is that you are actually craving something super healthy and lean without compromising flavor. Great for dessert or for breakfast, cold or warm, alone or with ice cream.

Heat oven to 350° F.

Line a baking sheet with parchment paper.

In a bowl, add pecans, oats, cinnamon and vanilla sugar. Mix well.

Place the apples on the baking sheet and fill each one with the mixture.

Pour wine into the center of the apples to keep the oat mixture moist. If you end up with extra wine, pour it into the baking sheet.

Bake for about 20-30 minutes. Serve warm or cold.

DATE, CHOCOLATE & NUT ROLLS

Yield

3 *rolls of cookies*

 GF

1	package of pitted dates (13 oz/375 g)
1	package of vegan semi-sweet chocolate (5 oz)
1 TSP	vanilla extract
1 TBSP	coconut oil
1 TBSP	pure maple syrup
2 TBSP	almond milk
1/3 C	roasted walnuts
1/3 C	roasted pistachio
1/3 C	roasted hazelnuts
1/3 C	sweetened coconut flakes

topping:

1/2 C	raw sesame seeds

Dates and chocolate are the best end to any type of meal. These bite-sized pieces melt in your mouth and satisfy that craving for sweets.

In a saucepan, add dates, chocolate, vanilla, coconut oil, pure maple syrup and almond milk.

Stir constantly on low heat until completely combined. Add walnuts, pistachios, hazelnuts, coconut flakes and stir.

Cut 3 pieces of aluminum foil, each about 12"x9". Sprinkle the foil with sesame seed. Divide the date mixture into thirds and spread each onto its respective foil sheet so it spans the entire length of the middle third of the foil. Fold the edges of the aluminum foil and roll tightly so it forms a log, approximately 1" in diameter. Twist the edges of the aluminum foil like a candy wrapper. Repeat for the other two rolls.

Freeze the rolls for a few hours, preferably overnight or until completely hardened.

Thinly slice bite-size pieces. You can keep in an airtight container in the freezer and serve when desired.

Yield

12-15 *cookies*

1 C	tahini paste
1 C	maple syrup
3/4 C	unsweetened coconut flakes
1/2 TSP	cinnamon
3 C	gf oats
1 C	walnuts, chopped

TAHINI OATMEAL COOKIES

Heat oven to 375° F.

Line a baking sheet with parchment paper.

In a bowl, mix tahini paste and maple syrup.

In another bowl, add coconut flakes, oats, cinnamon and walnuts.

Pour the dry ingredients into the wet ingredients and mix to combine. With an ice cream scoop, create evenly sized cookies. Bake for about 15 minutes, until the edges get golden brown.

Yield

10-12 *cookies*

3 C   raw sesame seeds,
       divided
2 C   sweet coconut flakes,
       divided
1/2 C pure maple syrup
1 TBSP vanilla sugar
  +   coconut oil spray

       glaze:

2 OZ   vegan semi-sweet
       chocolate
1/4 TSP coconut oil

HEART-SHAPED SESAME COOKIES

Sesame is a staple ingredient in Middle Eastern cooking and baking. It is used in everything from halva to tahini, and has endless health benefits.

Heat oven to 375° F.

Line a baking sheet with parchment paper and spray with coconut oil. Set aside.

In a food processor, add one cup sesame seeds, one cup coconut flakes, pure maple syrup and vanilla sugar. Blend for a few minutes until you have a paste. Pour into a bowl.

Add the rest of the coconut flakes and sesame seeds. Mix with a spatula. Pour onto a baking sheet and firmly press down using the spatula to spread the mixture evenly.

Bake for about 15-20 minutes, until golden brown.

In the meantime, put the chocolate in a small bowl and melt in the microwave. Add oil and mix.

Remove from the oven when the top of the cookie dough is golden brown and let cool in the pan.

Drizzle the chocolate with a fork to create a lined pattern.

Use a heart-shaped cookie cutter to cut the cookies, but do not try to separte them quite yet. Let them cool completely on a cooling rack, then separate the cookies.

You can also choose to cut the sheet into square cookies.

3	medium beets, peeled and steamed
1/3 C	coconut oil, melted
1 C	vanilla oat, soy, or almond milk
1 1/3 C	pure maple syrup
1 TSP	cinnamon
1 1/4 C	flour
1/4 TSP	salt
2 TBSP	cocoa powder
1 1/2 TSP	baking powder
1 C	chocolate chips

frosting:

1	vegan cream cheese (8 oz/227 g)
2 TBSP	coconut oil
+	zest of 1 lemon
+	juice of 1/2 lemon
3/4 C	powdered sugar

topping:

1 TBSP	cocoa powder
1 TBSP	sugar

These cupcakes have antioxidant-rich beets, which help detox your body and benefit heart health. They also contain coconut oil that not only enhances the flavors, but has good fats that regulate blood sugar.

RED VELVET CUPCAKES

Heat oven to 375° F.

In a food processor, add beets, coconut oil, milk and pure maple syrup. Blend until smooth. Pour into a mixing bowl.

In another mixing bowl, add cinnamon, flour, baking powder, salt and cocoa powder. Mix well.

Slowly pour the dry ingredients into the wet ingredients. Mix until the batter is incorporated and there are no lumps. Add the chocolate chips and mix with a spatula until they are evenly distributed.

Pour the mixture into a cupcake mold and bake in the oven for about 20 minutes. Check if they're done by inserting a toothpick into one of the cupcakes. If the toothpick comes out clean and dry, they're ready.

frosting:

Make sure the cheese and coconut oil are at room temperature.

Use a hand mixer to whip together all the ingredients until the desired consistency is reached. Pour the frosting into a piping bag.

After the cupcakes have cooled completely, frost and sprinkle with the cocoa-sugar mixture.

HAMENTASCHEN

Yield

28 *Hamentaschen (approx.)*

1 C	organic sprouted spelt flour
1 C	almond meal
2 TBSP	pure maple syrup
1 TSP	baking powder
1/2 C	coconut oil, melted
1/2 C	vanilla oat milk (or your favorite alternative)
+	pinch of salt

for the filling:

*	raspberry spread
2 OZ	vegan unsweetened chocolate
2 TBSP	vanilla oat milk
1/2 TSP	cinnamon
1 TBSP	pure maple syrup

topping:

+	powdered sugar

Heat oven to 375° F.

Line a baking sheet with parchment paper.

for the dough:

Add spelt flour, almond meal, pure maple syrup, baking powder, and pinch of salt to a food processor. Pulse a couple of times. Add coconut oil and milk. Mix until combined.

Dust your working surface with flour and roll the dough into a thin layer about 1/8" thick. Use a round cookie cutter (I used 2 5/8" diameter or 68 mm). Makes about 14 raspberry cookies and 12-14 chocolate cookies.

for the filling:

Put all the chocolate ingredients (chocolate, vanilla oat milk, cinnamon, pure maple syrup) in a glass bowl and microwave for one minute. Mix well and set aside.

preparation:

Use a spoon to add filling to the center of each cookie. Then pinch together one side and then the other 2 corners to create a triangle. You can pinch the dough so that it completely covers the filling or leave open with filling showing—it's up to you.

Bake in the oven for about 15-20 minutes or until golden brown.

Let cool completely. Sprinkle with powdered sugar and serve.

Hamentaschen are traditional Purim holiday cookies. This is a wonderful recipe for these soft cookies that literally melt in your mouth. No white flour is used, only healthy flours like almond meal and spelt flour.

"Mishloah manot" is the act of giving a basket with food items (usually containing Hamentaschen) as a show of kindness during Purim. With these Hamentaschen, you can be confident that you are spreading both health and joy to your friends and family.

Yield

4-6 *servings*

 (GF)

2 C	chickpeas, soaked overnight and drained
1 C	short grain brown rice
3 1/2 C	water
3 TBSP	pure maple syrup
1/2 TSP	salt

SWEET RICE & CHICKPEA DESSERT

This dessert is based on my Romanian grandmother's recipe, which she made for me all the time when I was a little girl.

There are so many ways to serve this dish. Traditionally or, if you want to add more flavors, include fresh berries, raspberry preserves, cinnamon, or some other favorite topping. You can serve it warm or cold.

Check out my tip on how to soak and cook beans (page 218).

Add all ingredients to a pot. Bring to a boil, then lower to a simmer and cook until all the water has evaporated and the chickpeas and rice are tender.

Serve as is or sprinkle with some cinnamon. You can also top with fresh berries or raspberry preserves.

Yield

10-12 *servings*

for the crust:

9	vegan graham crackers (4.8 oz/136 g)
1/2 C	slivered almonds
1 TBSP	coconut oil

filling:

+	zest of one lemon
1	package silken organic tofu (16 oz/454 g)
1 C	raw cashews, soaked overnight and drained
1	package vegan sour cream (12 oz/340 g)
1/2 TSP	vanilla extract
2 TSP	lemon juice
1/2 C	pure maple syrup
2 TSP	arrowroot

CITRUSY CHEESECAKE

This cheesecake is loaded with protein, is light in sugar, and tastes just like real cheesecake.

Heat oven to 350° F.

for the crust:

In a food processor, add all crust ingredients. Pulse until it gets to a sand-like texture. Pour into a 10" diameter round baking pan and press firmly down with your hands.

for the filling:

Add all ingredients to a clean food processor and process until super smooth.

preparation:

Pour filling onto the crust and bake for about 50 minutes.

Let cool and then place in the fridge for a few hours or overnight.

Decorate with your favorite fruits and serve chilled.

Yield

8-10 *servings*

6	pears, peeled, cored and steamed
1/4 C	brown sugar
2 TBSP	fresh lemon juice
3 OZ	fresh mint leaves, large bunch
1/4 C	brandy (optional)

PEAR & MINT GRANITA

This dessert is healthy, refreshing and perfect on a summer night.

Pears are naturally sweet and when combined with the freshness of mint, they create a lovely granita.

Tip: You can substitute the fresh pears with canned pears.

In a food processor, add all ingredients and blend until smooth.

Transfer to an airtight container and freeze. It will take about 8-10 hours until it is completely frozen. Every 2 hours use a fork to scrape the granita until it's nice and slushy.

Serve in a martini glass, garnish with a mint leaf and a cherry.

Yield

10-12 *servings*

1/2 C	coconut oil, melted
2	flax eggs (2 tablespoons flaxseed meal and 6 tablespoons water)
3/4 C	coconut palm sugar or brown sugar
1 TSP	baking powder
+	pinch of salt
1/2 C	cocoa powder
3/4 C	spelt flour

for serving:

+	powdered sugar

BROWNIES

These brownies are best at room temperature.

You can also bake in one pyrex dish and cut into squares. Baking time will be approximately 20 minutes.

Heat oven to 375° F.

In a mixing bowl, add coconut oil, sugar and flax eggs. Mix well until the sugar is dissolved.

In another mixing bowl, add baking powder, salt, cocoa powder and flour. Mix well.

Slowly add the dry ingredients to the wet ingredients and mix constantly until you reach a smooth texture.

Shape mixture into small balls with wet hands and place in bite-size baking cups. Bake for 10 minutes.

Let cool, sprinkle with powdered sugar and serve.

TAPIOCA PUDDING TOPPED WITH FRESH BERRIES

Yield

10-12 *cups*

1/3 C   tapioca pearls, not quick cook ones

2 C   water

1/3 C   maple syrup or agave or a combination of the two

1   can of coconut milk (13.5 oz/400 ml)

1/2 TSP   vanilla extract

1 TBSP   rose water

1/4 TSP   cardamom

for serving:

+   mixed fresh berries

Soak the tapioca pearls for 2-4 hours in water. Drain.

To a saucepan, add tapioca, water and agave/maple syrup. Bring to a boil and stir constantly. Add coconut milk and vanilla extract. Lower the heat to a simmer and keep stirring. Cook until the pearls have become large and clear in color and the pudding has become thick.

Add rose water and cardamom. Mix.

Pour into serving dishes and place in the fridge for about 2 hours or overnight. Decorate with berries or your favorite fruits and serve chilled.

Yield

10-12 *bites*

3/4 C	coconut milk
3/4 C	powdered sugar
2 C	shredded unsweetened coconut flakes

chocolate:

1	package vegan dark chocolate (8 oz/226 g)
1 TBSP	coconut oil
1 TSP	vanilla extract
2-3 TBSP	powdered sugar

BOUNTY BITES

In a mixing bowl, add coconut milk, sugar and coconut flakes. Mix well.

Line a baking sheet with parchment paper.

Use a small ice cream scoop to create mini coconut balls. Place on the baking sheet and refrigerate for 30 minutes.

In the meantime, melt chocolate in a double boiler or microwave. Add vanilla extract, powdered sugar and coconut oil. Mix well using a whisk.

Use a fork to dip each coconut ball into the melted chocolate and place back on the baking sheet. Refrigerate for 30 minutes.

Rewarm any leftover chocolate. Use a fork to drizzle the melted chocolate on top of the bites in a striped pattern. Let cool in the fridge for another half an hour.

Store in an airtight container and keep in the fridge or freezer.

Yield

10-12 *cookies*

1 C   flaxseed meal
1/2 C   almond flour
1/2 C   coconut flour
1 TSP   ground cinnamon
1/3 C   pure maple syrup
3/4 C   apple sauce

filling:

+ raspberry jam or any other kind that you like
+ powdered sugar to sprinkle on top

FLAXSEED SANDWICH COOKIES

Recently, I was looking for a way to use flaxseed meal in my baking. I experimented with several different dessert recipes, but the most successful one was for these soft flaxseed cookies. They melt in your mouth.

I love raspberry jam and it goes so well with these cookies. Another plus is they're gluten-free. They are much easier to digest, and the ingredients are very healthy.

Some people call flaxseed one of the most powerful plant foods on the planet. It is good for you in so many ways.

Heat oven to 375° F.

In a food processor, add all ingredients and pulse until completely incorporated into a dough.

Line a baking sheet with parchment paper.

Portion bite-sized cookies and press with a fork to create indentations.

Bake for about 15-20 minutes, until the edges become golden brown.

Let cool completely.

Make cookie sandwiches using a tablespoon of jam for filling. Make sure to leave the indented part of the cookie on the outside.

Sprinkle with powdered sugar and serve.

FRUIT SHAKE CAKE

Yield

10-12 *servings*

2 TBSP	coconut oil, melted
1 C	pure maple syrup
2 C	fruit shake of your choice (e.g. my Red Goodness Shake, page 12)
1 TSP	vanilla extract
2 C	spelt flour
1 1/2 TSP	baking soda
1 TSP	cinnamon

Heat oven to 350° F.

Grease a loaf pan with coconut oil.

In a mixing bowl, add coconut oil, pure maple syrup, fruit shake and vanilla extract. Mix well.

In another mixing bowl, add dry ingredients (flour, baking soda and cinnamon).

Pour the dry ingredients into the wet ingredients in small batches and whisk to a smooth texture.

Pour into the loaf pan and bake for about 40-50 minutes. Check if it's done by inserting a toothpick into the center of the cake. If it comes out dry and clean, it's done.

This cake is one of those coffee cakes that, visually, looks so simple but is actually full of complex flavors and healthy ingredients. Basically, you are in charge of the flavors. Whatever you like in your fruit shake will be used as the "wet ingredients" in your cake. For the one pictured I used my "Red Goodness Shake" (page 12), which contains beets, carrots, ginger, apple and more. All you need is a whisk and a mixing bowl and you are done.

Yield

6-8 *mini cups*

3 TBSP	chia seeds
1 C	vanilla soy or almond milk
3 TSP	pure maple syrup
1 TSP	cocoa powder
1/2 TSP	cinnamon

CHIA CHOCOLATE PUDDING

Chia seeds are considered a superfood because of their vast health benefits. I try to incorporate them into as much of my daily cooking as possible.

It is a good no-bake and no-hassle dessert.

Tip: If you prefer a smoother pudding, mix the pudding in a food processor to a texture of your liking.

In a mason jar, add all ingredients. Mix well and let soak overnight in the refrigerator. It's ready!

You can warm it up in the microwave for one minute and have a very nutritious breakfast. Or you can serve it as a dessert in small shot glasses. Decorate with dried coconut.

1 C almond flour
1 C peanut butter
1 flax egg, (1 tablespoon flaxseed meal mixed with 3 tablespoon of water)
1/2 C pure maple syrup
1 TBSP coconut oil

topping:

+ jam, your favorite kind

PEANUT BUTTER & JELLY COOKIES

These cookies are the ultimate example of a guilt-free treat. They are loaded with protein, low in sugar, contain good fat, and most importantly, are extremely delicious.

I like to use a raspberry jam on mine, but you can add any kind you like on yours.

Heat oven to 375° F.

Line a baking sheet with parchment paper. Set aside.

Mix all the dough ingredients in a food processor.

Create bite-sized balls with your hands and lay on the baking sheet. Create a dent with your thumb on each cookie and fill with jam.

Cook for about 10-15 minutes. Let cool and serve.

You can store them in an airtight container in the fridge for about a week.

Yield

12-14 *cookies*

2 C	gluten-free oat flour
1 TSP	baking powder
1 TSP	cinnamon
1/4 C	walnuts, chopped
1/2 C	date syrup
1 TSP	vanilla extract
1 C	boiling water
2 TBSP	coconut oil

DATE SYRUP SOFT BISCOTTI

These yummy, no added-sugar biscotti can be made soft or hard like the traditional ones. By "soft" I mean they're not baked again after slicing.

You can toast and spread them with your favorite jam.

Heat oven to 375° F.

In a bowl, add oat flour, baking powder, cinnamon and walnuts. Mix.

In another bowl, add date syrup, vanilla extract, boiling water and coconut oil. Mix with a whisk.

Add wet ingredients to the dry ingredients and mix.

Pour into a greased loaf pan and bake for about 25 minutes.

Optional: let it cool down, slice and bake again for about 10-15 minutes for extra crunch.

Yield

12-14 *squares*

 GF

1 C	corn flour
2 C	gluten-free oatmeal
1 TSP	baking powder
1/2 TSP	cinnamon
1/2 C	date syrup
1 C	almond milk
1/4 C	pure maple syrup
1/2 C	coconut oil, melted
1 C	dry roasted cashews
1 C	raspberry jam

OATMEAL SQUARES WITH RASPBERRY JAM

Oatmeal squares can be a guilt-free, gluten-free indulgence with your coffee. I like to use raspberry jam, but you can certainly use any of your other favorite jams. The oatmeal squares are soft and have some crunch from the cashews. Plus, there is no raw sugar in this recipe, which makes it even better.

Heat oven to 375° F.

In a mixing bowl, add corn flour, oatmeal, baking powder and cinnamon. Mix.

In another bowl, add date syrup, almond milk and pure maple syrup. Mix well.

Slowly add the wet ingredients to the dry ingredients, mixing constantly. Add the coconut oil and mix well. Then add the cashews and mix.

Cover the bottom of a baking sheet with half of the mixture, pressing firmly to flatten the

mixture. Spread the raspberry jam on top then cover with the remaining mixture. Bake in the oven for about 30-35 minutes.

Cut into squares and place in individual ziplock bags for a grab-and-go snack.

ALMOND BUTTER & CHOCOLATE CHIP COOKIES

Yield

30 *cookies*	

2 C organic gf flour blend
1 TSP baking powder
2 flax eggs, (mix 2 tablespoons flaxseed meal + 6 tablespoons of water. Let sit for 10-15 minutes.)
1 C almond butter
1/2 C almond milk
1/2 C pure maple syrup
1/2 C vegan chocolate chips

topping:

+ powdered sugar

Heat oven to 375° F.

In a mixing bowl, add flour and baking powder. Set aside.

In another bowl add flax eggs, almond butter, almond milk and pure maple syrup. Mix well.

Slowly pour the dry ingredients into the wet ingredients and mix until blended. Add the chocolate chips.

Roll the dough into a log then wrap in plastic wrap. You can create two logs if it's easier. Freeze the dough for an hour or overnight.

Line a baking sheet with parchment paper. With a sharp knife, slice the dough into cookies, about 1/2" or 3/4" thick. Bake for about 15-20 minutes. Let cool.

Dust with powdered sugar and serve.

These cookies are somewhere between muffins and cookies.

Yield

13-15 *muffins*

3 bananas, mashed
1/3 C almond milk
3/4 C pure maple syrup
1/3 C coconut oil, melted
1 C corn flour
1/2 C almond flour
1 TSP baking powder
1 TSP baking soda
+ pinch of salt

BANANA MUFFINS

Tip: If you have ripe bananas but don't have time to use them in a recipe, peel them and store in a ziplock bag in the freezer. When you are ready to bake, just take them out of the freezer, thaw, and use.

Heat oven to 375° F.

In a mixing bowl, add bananas, almond milk, pure maple syrup and coconut oil. Mix well.

In another bowl, add corn flour, almond flour, baking powder, baking soda and salt. Mix well.

Slowly pour the dry ingredients into the wet ingredients and whisk to combine.

Line a muffin tin with baking cups. Use a spoon to distribute evenly sized portions of batter into the baking cups. Bake for about 30 minutes. Let cool before serving.

Yield

16-17 *hamentaschen*

1/4 TSP xanthan gum
1/4 C arrowroot flour
1/2 C almond flour
1/2 C gluten-free oat flour
1/4 C coconut flour
1/4 C coconut oil
1/4 C maple syrup

filling:

+ dairy-free and gluten-free chocolate chips

CHOCOLATE CHIP HAMENTASCHEN

Heat oven to 375° F.

Line a baking sheet with parchment paper.

In a food processor, first add all dry ingredients: xanthan gum, arrowroot, almond flour and coconut flour. Pulse a couple of times. Then add the wet ingredients: coconut oil and maple syrup. Process for a minute or less, until the dough is formed.

Dust your working surface and the rolling pin with flour. Roll the dough into a 1/8" thick layer.

Use a round cookie cutter or cup to cut the dough. Place a teaspoon of chocolate chips in the center of each cookie. Pinch three sides of the circle to create a triangle shape. See picture above. Place on the cookie sheet.

Bake for about 10-15 minutes.

Let cool, sprinkle with powdered sugar and serve.

MANGO BLACK STICKY RICE

Yield

6-8 *servings*   GF

1 C   black rice/forbidden rice
2 1/2 C   water
1   can light coconut milk
       (14 oz/400 ml), divided
+   pinch of salt
4 TBSP pure maple syrup

topping:

1   mango, sliced
+   sweetened coconut
       flakes

In a pot, add rice, water, salt, pure maple syrup and 1 cup coconut milk. Bring to a boil, then reduce to a simmer for about 45 minutes.

Add the rest of the coconut milk and cook for about 10 more minutes or until you reach the consistency of a pudding.

Let cool, pour into a serving bowl, add mango on top, and sprinkle with coconut flakes.

Mango sticky rice is one of my favorite desserts and snacks. I love the combination of the slightly sweet rice pudding with the freshness of the mango.

This is an easy recipe with a twist on traditional white sticky rice. (You can certainly use white sticky rice instead of black rice if you prefer.)

Yield

10-12 *servings*

filling:

1 C	raw cashews, soaked overnight and drained
1 C	pumpkin purée
1 C	pure maple syrup
1	package organic sprouted tofu (14 oz/397 g)
+	zest and juice of 1 lemon
1/4 TSP	cinnamon
1/4 TSP	all spice
1/4 TSP	nutmeg

crust:

1/2 C	almond flour
1 C	candied pecans
1/4 C	coconut oil

When pumpkin cheesecake is on the menu, it means it's holiday season. This cheesecake is very flavorful, mildly spiced, decadent, but not too sweet. I used candied pecans for the crust, which added another texture and another layer of flavor. You can also make this recipe in individual ramekins for a more elegant presentation.

PUMPKIN CHEESECAKE

Heat oven to 375° F.

filling:

In a food processor, add cashews, pumpkin purée, pure maple syrup, tofu, lemon juice, cinnamon, all spice and nutmeg. Blend until very smooth. Set aside.

crust:

In a food processor, add almond flour, pecans and coconut oil. Pulse until combined.

In a 10" diameter round baking dish, add the crust mixture and press down on it firmly. Pour the filling on top.

Bake for about 40-50 minutes. Let cool and serve chilled.

Yield

6-8 *servings*

1 package shredded pastry dough (8 oz/226 g)
6-8 TBSP coconut oil, melted
6-8 TBSP raw brown sugar

filling:

1 C frozen blueberries, thawed and drained
1 package vegan cream cheese (8 oz/227 g)
6-7 leaves of fresh mint
1 lemon, zest and juice
3 TBSP pure maple syrup
1/3 C cashews, soaked overnight and drained

topping:

1/4 C pistachios, roasted, salted and chopped
6 strawberries, cut into small pieces

PURPLE CHEESECAKE ON SHREDDED PASTRY

We all eat with our eyes first, so a colorful dish such as this creates a gourmet essence.

Shredded pastries are very common in Middle Eastern cuisine. You can find the shredded dough in the freezer section of most Mediterranean grocery stores.

Heat oven to 375° F.

Using your hands, fill 6-8 baking cups with the shredded dough. Then pour 1 teaspoon of coconut oil in each cup, and try to spread it as much as possible. Sprinkle 1 teaspoon of raw sugar on each cup.

Bake in the oven for about 20 minutes or until the edges get golden brown.

Remove from the oven and let cool on a cooling rack.

filling:

In a food processor, add blueberries, cream cheese, mint, lemon, pure maple syrup and cashews. Mix until very smooth. Place in the fridge to set and cool.

Assemble just before serving, or the pastry will get soggy.

Take a few spoonfuls of the filling and place in each pastry cup. Sprinkle with pistachio and strawberries and serve.

Acknowledgements

I wanted to thank a few people that helped make this book happen. To my wonderful graphic designer Kristin McCleerey, who professionally and patiently made this book tangible. Second, a big thank you to my husband Rany. Without his support, I could not have done this at all. Next, many thanks to my daughter Orian who spent countless hours making this book a dream come true for me. To my boys Roy and Carmel, I am so proud of your creative minds—you bring so much joy to my life! To my parents, my biggest fans, thank you for your unconditional love and support and for always believing in me. I love you all!

Index

A

C

Butter Beans & Quinoa Veggie Stew
120
Tshulent 124
TVP Kebab over Tahini & Cauliflower
Steak 136
Tamales 137
Mushroom Kibbeh 141
Mac & Cheese 156

PAPRIKA PASTE
Dried Pea Patties in Picante Red Sauce
104

PARSLEY
Hummus 29
Baked Falafel 46
Tomatoes, Peppers, Cilantro & Parsley
55
Moroccan Chickpeas 58
Country-Style Soup 63
Chanterelle Mushrooms & Rutabaga
Soup 69
Kneidlach (Matzo Ball) Soup 74
Rice Salad 75
Cauliflower Salad Stuffed Tomatoes 78
Israeli Salad with Quinoa 79
Bulgur Tabbouleh Salad 82
Sumac-Spiced Spinach & Veggie Salad
83
Parsley Pear Salad 87
Mushroom Bulgur Burgers 98
Brown Rice & Black Bean Burgers 99
Superfood Veggie Patties 101
Dried Pea Patties in Picante Red Sauce
104
Black & Brown Rice Balls over Zucchini
& Garbanzo Beans 111
Stuffed Peppers 113
Chanterelle & Portobello Mushroom
Ragout over Red Lentil Purée
121
TVP Kebab over Tahini & Cauliflower
Steak 136

PARSNIP
Country-Style Soup 63
Corn, Chestnut & Coconut Soup 67
Black-Eyed Pea Soup 70
Decadent Eggplant Soup 71
Butter Beans & Quinoa Veggie Stew
120
Baked & Stuffed Yams 143
Creamy Parsnip Purée over Pasta 160

PASTA
Zucchini Spaghetti 153
Roasted Red Pepper & Tomato Pasta
155
Mac & Cheese 156
Roasted Vegetable Lasagna 157
Spinach Pesto Pasta 159
Creamy Parsnip Purée over Pasta 160
Yam Gnocchi in Almond Sage
Sauce 161
Kreplach 163
Stir Fry Veggies over Buckwheat
Noodles 164

PEANUT BUTTER
Thai Curry Soup 73
Salad Rolls with Warm Peanut Sauce
90
Peanut Butter & Jelly Cookies 186

PEAR
Energy Boost Shake 11
Breakfast Green Shake 13
Parsley Pear Salad 87
Pear & Mint Granita 177

PEARL BARLEY
Stuffed Peppers 113
Eggplant Rolls 115
Tshulent 124

PEAS
Mediterranean Tofu Bowl 130
Shepherd's Pie topped with
Cauliflower Purée 145

PECANS
Baked Green Apples 168

PECANS, CANDIED
Pumpkin Cheesecake 195

PEPPERONCINIS
Fresh Green Chickpea Spread 56

PINE NUTS
Winter Greens Salad with Beets,
Pomelo & Pine Nuts 85
Tomato Basil Salad 86

PINTO BEANS
Roasted Chickpeas & Roasted Pinto
Beans 51
Pinto Bean Salad 52
Sumac-Spiced Spinach & Veggie Salad
83

Shepherd's Pie topped with
Cauliflower Purée 145

PISTACHIOS
Date, Chocolate & Nut Rolls 169
Purple Cheesecake on Shredded
Pastry 196

PLUM
Chopped Raw Brussels Sprout, Apple &
Dried Plum Salad 81

POLENTA
Dried Pea Patties in Picante Red Sauce
104
Roasted Tower 139

POMELO
Winter Greens Salad with Beets,
Pomelo & Pine Nuts 85

POTATO
Creamy Potato Soup topped with
Black Beans 65
Kneidlach (Matzo Ball) Soup 74
Mac & Cheese 156

POWDERED SUGAR
Cheese Blintzes 17
Chocolate Banana Bread 167
Red Velvet Cupcakes 172
Hamentaschen 173
Brownies 178
Bounty Bites 181
Flaxseed Sandwich Cookies 182
Almond Butter & Chocolate Chip
Cookies 189

PUFF PASTRY
Puff Pastry Burek filled with Feta
Cheese & Olives 37
Asparagus Wrapped In Puff Pastry 50

PUMPKIN
Pumpkin Pancakes 15
Baked Mini Pumpkin with Couscous &
Garbanzo Beans 123
Roasted Vegetable Lasagna 157
Pumpkin Cheesecake 195

QUICHE
Broccoli Quiche 22

Creamy Potato Soup topped with
    Black Beans 65
Zucchini & Pearl Barley Soup 66
Corn, Chestnut & Coconut Soup 67
Cooked Fresh Beans 68
Chanterelle Mushrooms & Rutabaga
    Soup 69
Black-Eyed Pea Soup 70
Decadent Eggplant Soup 71
Indian-Style Black Lentil Soup 72
Thai Curry Soup 73
Kneidlach (Matzo Ball) Soup 74

SOY CURLS
Spicy Soy Curl Chraime 132
Soy Curls Shawarma 140

SOY MILK
Cheese Blintzes 17
Tofu Omelet 20
Mac & Cheese 156
Red Velvet Cupcakes 172

SOY SAUCE
Corn, Chestnut & Coconut Soup 67
Thai Curry Soup 73
Asian Cabbage Slaw 91
Tofu & Veggie Patties 95
Hot Dogs 100
Baked Corn Schnitzel 105
Butternut Squash stuffed with
    Mushrooms & Crunchy Tofu
    117
Shishito Peppers over Crunchy Tofu &
    Broccoli 149

SPELT
Spelt & Black Lentil Majadra 126

SPELT FLOUR
Pumpkin Pancakes 15
Cheese Blintzes 17
Heart-Shaped Mini Zucchini Cakes 19
Homemade Cereal 25
Beer Bread 42
Baked Corn Schnitzel 105
Chanterelle & Portobello Mushroom
    Ragout over Red Lentil Purée
    121
Yam Gnocchi in Almond Sage
    Sauce 161
Chocolate Banana Bread 167
Hamentaschen 173
Brownies 178
Fruit Shake Cake 183

SPINACH
Spinach Casserole 16
Sumac-Spiced Spinach & Veggie Salad
    83
Winter Greens Salad with Beets,
    Pomelo & Pine Nuts 85
Butter Beans & Quinoa Veggie Stew
    120
Stuffed Eggplant 147
Spinach Pesto Pasta 159

SPLIT PEAS, YELLOW
Hot Dogs 100

SRIRACHA HOT SAUCE
Sesame Crusted Tofu over Peas &
    Spinach 118

STRAWBERRIES
Cheese Blintzes 17
Purple Cheesecake on Shredded
    Pastry 196

SUN DRIED TOMATO
Cocktail Meat(less) Balls 41
Stuffed Chard Leaves 133

SUNFLOWER SEEDS
Gluten-Free Biscuits 24
Oat Crackers 53
Roasted Butternut Squash & Ginger
    Soup 64
Parsley Pear Salad 87

SWEET CHILI SAUCE
Celery Salad 77
Salad Rolls with Warm Peanut Sauce
    90
Asian Cabbage Slaw 91
Sesame Crusted Tofu over Peas &
    Spinach 118
Butter Beans & Quinoa Veggie Stew
    120
Stuffed Cabbage 135
Shishito Peppers over Crunchy Tofu &
    Broccoli 149
Spicy Eggplant Curry 150
Stir Fry Veggies over Buckwheat
    Noodles 164

SWEET POTATO
Superfood Veggie Patties 101
Kreplach 163

SWEETENED COCONUT FLAKES
Date, Chocolate & Nut Rolls 169
Tahini Oatmeal Cookies 170
Heart-Shaped Sesame Cookies 171
Mango Black Sticky Rice 193

T

TAHINI
Hummus 29
Black Lentil Dip 30
Roasted Eggplant with Tahini & Date
    Syrup 34
Tahini Sauce 46
Baked Falafel 46
Pink Tahini over Roasted Eggplant 48
Fresh Green Chickpea Spread 56
Baked Corn Schnitzel 105
Tahini Oatmeal Cookies 170

TAMARI
Sesame Crusted Tofu over Peas &
    Spinach 118
Indian Red Lentil & Azuki Dahl over
    Brown Rice 128

TAPIOCA PEARLS
Tapioca Pudding topped with Fresh
    Berries 179

THYME
Mushroom Bulgur Burgers 98
Brown Rice & Black Bean Burgers 99
Butternut Squash stuffed with
    Mushrooms & Crunchy Tofu
    117

TOFU
Spinach Casserole 16
Cheese Blintzes 17
Tofu Omelet 20
Broccoli Quiche 22
Thai Curry Soup 73
Salad Rolls with Warm Peanut Sauce
    90
Tofu & Veggie Patties 95
Baked Corn Schnitzel 105
Butternut Squash stuffed with
    Mushrooms & Crunchy Tofu
    117
Sesame Crusted Tofu over Peas &
    Spinach 118
Mediterranean Tofu Bowl 130

U

V

IN ESTEE'S *Pantry*

REFRIGERATOR

Tempeh
Tofu
Almond milk

FRESH PRODUCE

Avocado
Kale
Apple
Banana
Ginger root
Turmeric root
Lemon
Onion
Spring onion
Garlic
Cucumber
Pepper
Tomato
Red bell peppers
Cabbage, purple and white

BAKING

Vegan dark chocolate
Vegan graham crackers
Dates
Apple sauce
Cocoa powder
Unsweetened coconut flakes
Sesame seeds, white and black
Vanilla extract
Baking powder
Baking soda

CONDIMENTS

Dijon mustard
Miso paste white and red
Vegetable base
No chicken base
Tahini
Tamari
Soy sauce
Vegan mayonnaise

CANNED GOODS

Tomato paste
Tomato sauce
Crushed tomatoes
Light Coconut milk
Olives

RAW NUTS

Cashews
Almonds
Brazil Nuts
Walnuts
Pecans
Peanut butter
Almond butter

RICE, PASTA, FLOURS, GRAINS AND BEANS

GF Panko breadcrumbs
Brown rice
Basmati rice
Black rice
Pearl barley
Spelt
Quinoa
Tricolor quinoa
Green buckwheat
Roasted buckwheat
Chia seeds
GF steel cut oats
GF old fashioned oats
Flaxseed meal
Hemp seeds
Polenta

Seasoned seaweed
Garbanzo bean flour
Coconut flour
Almond flour
Spelt flour
White flour
GF flour blend
Arrowroot flour
Rice flour
GF oat flour
Tapioca flour
Masa harina flour
Xanthan gum
Soy curls
TVP
Bulgur
Kidney beans
Black beans
Lima beans
Pinto beans
White / great northern beans
Mung beans
Green lentils
Black lentils
Red lentils
Garbanzo beans
Dried green peas
Yellow split peas
Spaghetti
Rice noodles
GF lasagna noodles

SWEETENERS

Pure maple syrup
Date syrup
Date sugar
Brown sugar
Agave
Coconut sugar

OILS & VINEGARS

Extra virgin olive oil
Coconut oil
Balsamic vinegar
Apple cider vinegar
Rice vinegar

SPICES

Shawarma spice mix
Cayenne pepper
Chili flakes
Chili powder
Turmeric
Cumin
Cinnamon
Curry powder
Garam masala
Sumac
Cardamom
Zaatar
Sweet paprika
Smoked paprika
Garlic powder
Onion powder
Nutmeg
Old bay seasoning
Nigella seeds
Nutritional yeast

TOOLS

Food processor
Blender such as a Vitamix
Immersion blender

COOKING
Tips

DRIED BEANS

Using dried beans in recipes is quite common in the vegan diet. It can be intimidating if you don't know how to do it. Although it may sound complicated, you'll find that it's the easiest thing to do, and if you use my tips on how to do it, you'll save money (it's a lot cheaper to use dried beans versus canned beans) and it's a lot healthier to use dried beans versus canned since they don't contain any added preservatives. So, what I like to do is buy all kind of beans—from kidney beans, to black beans, to Lima beans to whatever else I find on the shelf. Try to choose organic beans since it's so inexpensive anyways—invest a few dollars more and avoid unnecessary chemicals that exist in non-organic beans. Store the dried beans in your pantry at all times. Next thing you are going to do, is you are going to take a package of the dried beans, (about 2 cups) and pour them into a large mixing bowl, then cover the beans with water all the way to the top of the mixing bowl, (a lot of water). Approximately 24 hours later, you'll strain the beans under running water, and store them in freezer ziplock bags. When ready to cook your beans, you'll take them out of the freezer and use in the recipe. It will shorten the cooking time and side effect from beans (some people may experience bloating and gas) drastically. In most of the recipes in the book, when I refer the measurements to beans, it will be after the beans have been soaked. There isn't a huge change in size from beans that have been soaked or cooked, however, there is a big change in size between dried beans and soaked/cooked beans.

COOKING DRIED BEANS

First, soak beans as directed above. When cooking beans, you simply need to add beans to a pot, cover with 3x the amount of water, add some salt, (similar to pasta) and cook until tender, then drain and use in a recipe, (only if the recipe calls for soaked, drained, and cooked beans). Some of the recipes will call for soaked and drained beans, and some of the recipes will call for soaked, drained and cooked beans.

SALT & PEPPER

You'll find that salt and pepper in most of the recipes will almost never specify an amount. The reason for it, is that salt and pepper are added to food according to your liking to enhance flavor. Some people like their food saltier and spicier than others, so add salt and pepper to taste.

"What is done in love is done well."

- Vincent Van Gogh